NEC3: The Role of the *Supervisor*

NEC3: The Role of the *Supervisor*

Institution of Civil Engineers
publishing

NEC3: The Role of the *Supervisor*

Bronwyn Mitchell and Barry Trebes

Published by ICE Publishing, One Great George Street, Westminster, London SW1P 3AA

Full details of ICE Publishing sales representatives and distributors can be found at:
www.icevirtuallibrary.com/printbooksales

Also available from ICE Publishing:

Managing Reality series, 2nd edition (5 volumes).
B Mitchell and B Trebes. ISBN 978-0-7277-3397-9
NEC3: A User's Guide: Engineering and Construction Contract.
J Broome. ISBN 978-0-7277-4109-7
NEC3 Practical Solutions.
RA Gerrard and S Kings. ISBN 978-0-7277-5969-6

www.icevirtuallibrary.com

A catalogue record for this book is available from the British Library

ISBN 978-0-7277-6096-8

© Thomas Telford 2015

ICE Publishing is a division of Thomas Telford Ltd, a wholly owned subsidiary of the Institution of
Civil Engineers (ICE).

Content reproduced with kind permission from *NEC3: How to Use the ECC Communication Forms*
(ISBN 978-0-7277-5909-2), available at www.neccontract.com.

Commissioning Editor: Amber Thomas
Development Editor: Maria Inês Pinheiro
Production Editor: Rebecca Casebourne
Market Development Executive: Elizabeth Hobson

Typeset by Academic + Technical, Bristol
Index created by Nigel D'Auvergne
Printed and bound in Great Britain by CPI Group (UK) Ltd, Croydon, CR0 4YY

Contents

About the authors

Bronwyn Mitchell, BCom (Hons), BProc, MBA, MCIPS, MCIArb, has been working with the NEC since 1995. Bronwyn drafted an NEC web page, which she sold to Thomas Telford Ltd in 1996. She assisted in redrafting a Small Works Contract, also written under licence, for Scottish contracting situations and this version was fundamentally adopted and later published as the Short Contract. She has worked with the ECC, ECSC, TSC, TSSC, PSC and PSSC as an advisor and trainer, providing guidance to both Parties and is co-author of *Managing Reality*.

Barry Trebes, BSc (Hons), MSc, FRICS, FAPM, FInstCES, has over 30 years' experience of providing consultancy, advice, facilitation and training on major developments across numerous business sectors, including aviation, defence, power, utilities, infrastructure, property, rail, highway and water, both in the UK and internationally. Barry provides NEC3 training and education, including providing NEC3 for Thomas Telford Master Classes and their Project Manager Accreditation course. He actively contributes to industry knowledge through numerous articles and is co-author of 'Managing Reality', a five-book set on the practical use of the NEC3 ECC contract, and BS PD 6079 part 4: *Guide to Project Management in the Construction Industry*. He also initiated and helped to develop the first web-based NEC3 contract management system, named CCM, with MPS Ltd in 2000.

Foreword

I was delighted to be asked to write a foreword for this book because of both the authors and the subject matter it involves. The *Supervisor* primarily features in the NEC3 Engineering and Construction Contract but also in the NEC3 Engineering and Construction Subcontract. Although the *Supervisor*'s responsibilities are considerably less extensive than perhaps the *Project Manager*, the role is no less important in contributing to meeting the *Employer*'s objectives on a project.

The main aim of this book is to guide *Supervisors* (or potential *Supervisors*) through their responsibilities – covering what they should do and what they should not do in undertaking the role effectively. This not only includes a good understanding of the express terms of the contract but deals with other areas that the *Supervisor* might get involved in and also sets out the necessary cultural aspects of being a competent *Supervisor*.

The term *Supervisor* is one of the few named in the contract and most people will naturally compare this to a more traditional clerk of works role. These roles are different and it's important that this is grasped. The *Supervisor* role is limited but proactive; technical of necessity, but practical too. People acting in this role should get a good understanding of its implications before they undertake it.

There are no other substantial texts that deal with the role of the *Supervisor* so the benefits and importance of this book are clear. It is of course helpful that the book is authoritative and well laid out in a chronological order. The timing of this book is also extremely relevant as it coincides with the introduction from NEC of a series of accreditations for the various roles under the NEC3 contracts. More details on the ECC Supervisor Accreditation can be found on www.neccontract.com, and I would urge anyone acting in that role, or clients wishing to appoint someone in that role, to give consideration to getting accredited or using accredited *Supervisors* on their projects.

Following on from their highly credible 'Managing Reality' series of books, Bronwyn Mitchell and Barry Trebes have co-written this book in their own simple and incredibly helpful style. The extensive experience of NEC contracts that they both have is obvious, and I cannot think of two better authors to have written this book.

Better and more informed *Supervisors* can only contribute to a better industry. I hope that you enjoy this book as much as I did.

Robert Alan Gerrard
NEC Users' Group Secretary

Abbreviations and other writing conventions used in this book

Abbreviations

ECC   NEC3 Engineering and Construction Contract
NEC3   New Engineering Contract (third edition)
QMS   quality management system
TQA   technical query and answer

Other writing conventions

- This book is designed as an effective companion to the NEC3 *Supervisor* training courses available through NEC, including ECC Supervisor Accreditation. It provides complementary information and, as such, much material is taken directly from the ECC.
- *How to Write the ECC Works Information* refers to the NEC's www.neccontract.com, *How to Write the ECC Works Information*, 2013, Thomas Telford, London.
- *How to Communicate* refers to the NEC's www.neccontract.com, *How to Use the ECC Communications Forms*, 2013, Thomas Telford, London.
- Site (capital S) has been used except where the word is part of another entity or description, such as site diary and site hut.
- Clauses pertaining to the *Supervisor*, and particularly those mentioned in sections 4 and 5, are detailed in Appendix 7B.
- Throughout the book there are shaded 'practical tip' boxes that immediately point the user towards important reminders for using the ECC. There are also unshaded boxes that contain key messages and examples to illustrate the text.
- Words importing the masculine gender only shall include the feminine gender and vice versa as applicable.

Section 1

NEC3: The Role of the *Supervisor*
ISBN 978-0-7277-6096-8

Introduction

The *Supervisor* is one of the key people involved in the NEC3 Engineering and Construction Contract (ECC). Other key people (named in the contract) are the *Project Manager*, the *Employer*, the *Contractor* and the *Adjudicator*. These other key people have descriptions that generally lead to a quick understanding of their role in the contract; for example, most people would know that the *Project Manager* is the person who undertakes the duties required to manage the contract to deliver the *Employer*'s project objectives.

The description '*Supervisor*' is not as easy to understand. Does the *Supervisor* supervise the contract and, if so, what does that entail? Users familiar with other forms of contract may try to fit the role of *Supervisor* into the frame provided by those other contracts and may, for example, equate the *Supervisor* with the clerk of works or the supervising officer/site agent in other contracts. However, the roles are not exactly the same and it is vital to understand the differences and the full effect of the *Supervisor* role in the ECC.

The *Contractor* is responsible for the achievement of the *Employer*'s quality objectives as set out in the Works Information. The *Supervisor* in his role, as far as possible, ensures that these quality objectives are being met by the *Contractor*.

The *Employer* may only involve the *Supervisor* as the *Contractor* starts on Site; but it must be recognised that a *Supervisor* can add value from project inception, and will certainly add value during the drafting of the documents that will form part of an invitation to tender to bidders.

The number of clauses in the ECC that refer to the *Supervisor* is small; however, there is a web of actions and requirements that support these clauses. This book provides the information every *Supervisor* needs to carry out his role fully.

Overview of this book
This book provides guidelines to those who have been allocated the role of *Supervisor* on an ECC contract by describing the obligations, activities and culture to fulfil the role effectively. The book is designed to be an effective companion to the ICE NEC3 *Supervisor* training course and provides complementary information.

The book describes the technical and behavioural traits that will be of use to the *Supervisor* and is divided into a chronological set of learning outcomes, as shown in Figure 1.1, that mirror the order in which a project can be established and implemented.

Figure 1.1 *Supervisor* book structure

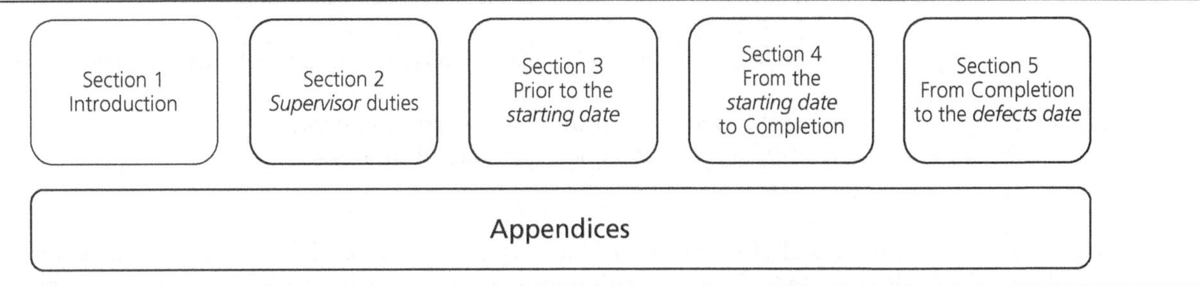

1.1.   Introducing the *Supervisor*
1.1.1   Glossary of terms
Glossary

The terminology used in the ECC and which is part of the *Supervisor*'s vocabulary in carrying out his required actions under the contract is included as Appendix 7B of this book.

Comparison of terms with other contracts

Table 1.1 lists some of the terms in the ECC, and the equivalent terms in other forms of contract with which those new to the ECC may be more familiar. The compared terms are not necessarily used in exactly the same way in all contracts.

Table 1.1 Comparison of terms between contracts

NEC3	Traditional contracts
Defect	Snags, snagging, punch list
Completion	Practical completion/substantial completion
period between Completion and the *defects date*	Defects Liability Period
defects date	End of the Defects Liability Period
Equipment	Constructional plant and things used to provide the works, for example, temporary works, etc.
take over	Handover/handback

1.1.2   Role of the *Supervisor*: main duties

A more detailed discussion of the clauses affecting the *Supervisor* is included in sections 3, 4 and 5 of this book. As a summary, the main duties of the *Supervisor* in the ECC are listed in Table 1.2.

Table 1.2 The main duties of the *Supervisor*

General duties	Defects	Tests and inspections	Marking
Act as stated in the contract and in a spirit of mutual trust and co-operation	Notify Defects and carry out searches	Watch tests and inspections carried out by the *Contractor*	Mark for payment purposes Equipment, Plant and Materials outside the Working Areas
Communicate and issue documents as required by the ECC3	Take account of Defects at Completion and the *defects date*	Carry out *Supervisor* tests and inspections and notify the *Contractor* of the results	

1.1.3   Principles of good project management
Project management

The principles of good project management can be employed by all parties and individuals who participate in the project and the contract – they are not restricted to the *Project Manager* of the ECC contract (see Figure 1.2). For example, three of the project management principles that affect the *Supervisor* are:

- Defined roles and responsibilities – the *Supervisor* role is clearly described in the ECC, as are the other roles in the contract
- Managing by exception – managing the Defect notification and correction process
- Quality control – for example, quality review techniques, tests and inspections, etc.

Skills of the *Supervisor*

The *Supervisor* needs some different skills from the *Project Manager* as his role is different and his interactions with the other roles in the ECC are also different. However, both roles require similar interpersonal skills, for communicating

Figure 1.2 Project management triangle

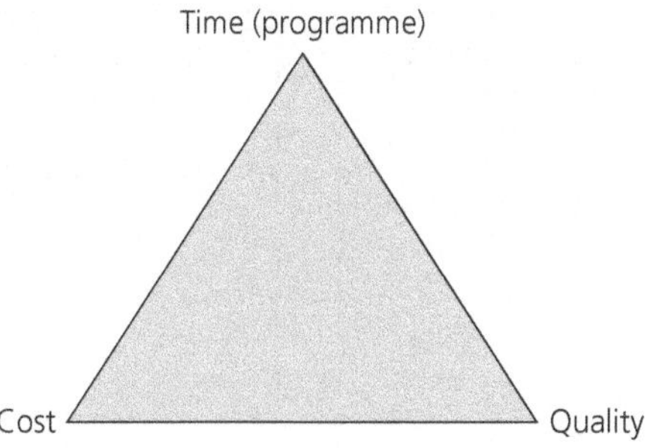

The *Supervisor*'s role focuses on one corner of the project management triangle: quality; although his actions may affect the time and cost points as well. The *Project Manager*'s understanding of the role of the *Supervisor* and that he [the *Project Manager*] is still responsible for the quality of the project affects his management of the contract, and may also impact on its outcome.

with key stakeholders and Others (clause 11.2(10)), investigating issues and working with the *Contractor* rather than against him.

The *Supervisor* should be proactive in the management of his actions so that he brings his role to life. He should put in place working practices that will enable him to undertake his role in the contract successfully. Good interpersonal skills are also required to be a success in the role of *Supervisor* as he will interact with other people every day, such as the *Project Manager*, the *Contractor*, Subcontractors, the *Employer* and day visitors to the Site (for example, inspectors).

It is worth emphasising that successful projects don't just happen; they are reliant on the people carrying out the contractual roles and the processes required by the contract. The ECC defines the process but people make the difference, and the *Supervisor* plays a key role in behaving in a collaborative culture and working with the wider project team.

Table 1.3 The good and bad habits of the *Supervisor* role

Good habits	Bad habits
■ Act as stated ■ Use the contract ■ Familiarise yourself with the contract ■ Communicate ■ Capture and share learning ■ State the reasons for your actions (for example, why it is a Defect) ■ Work collaboratively	■ Not acting as stated ■ Not notifying Defects ■ Waiting for the *Contractor* to notify you ■ Late management of Defects ■ Local 'work around'

1.1.4 Who is the *Supervisor*?

The ECC *Supervisor*

> The *Supervisor* is one of the named roles in the ECC and is required to carry out specific duties under the contract, such as testing and the inspection of Plant and Materials.

The *Supervisor* is one of the named roles in the ECC (see Figure 1.3). The other named roles are:

■ the *Employer*
■ the *Contractor*
■ the *Project Manager*
■ the *Adjudicator* (should be named in the Contract Data).

Where is the *Supervisor* named?

The *Supervisor* is identified in the Contract Data. In some cases the Contract Data may simply state the name of an organisation to which the *Employer* is outsourcing the role of the *Supervisor*; however, it is important that the *Employer* approves the person assigned the role and that the *Employer* notifies the name and contact details of the *Supervisor* to the *Contractor* prior to the *starting date* of the contract. In larger projects the *Project Manager* may be part of the panel that appoints the *Supervisor* so that he is comfortable with the personalities on the *Employer*'s team.

Figure 1.3 Who is the *Supervisor*

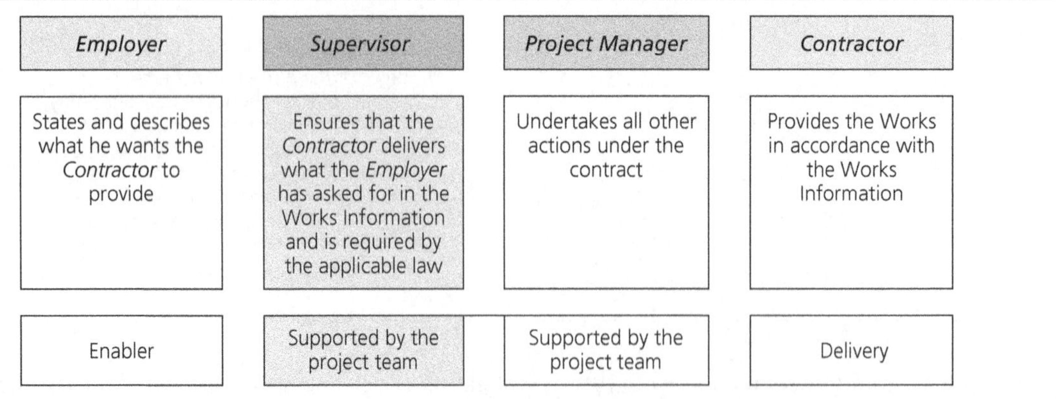

Appointing a *Supervisor*	As with any other project member, the sooner the *Supervisor* is appointed and starts working with the rest of the team and the documents which are relevant to the project, the better his knowledge and the more effective his contribution will be. A *Supervisor* who has been involved in a project since its business need was first identified will be in a better position to add value than one who is introduced post-commencement.
Replacing the *Supervisor*	The *Employer* may replace the *Supervisor* after he has notified the *Contractor* (clause 14.4).

Figure 1.4 shows an example of role differentiation in the *Employer*'s organisation.

Figure 1.4 Role differentiation in the *Employer*'s organisation

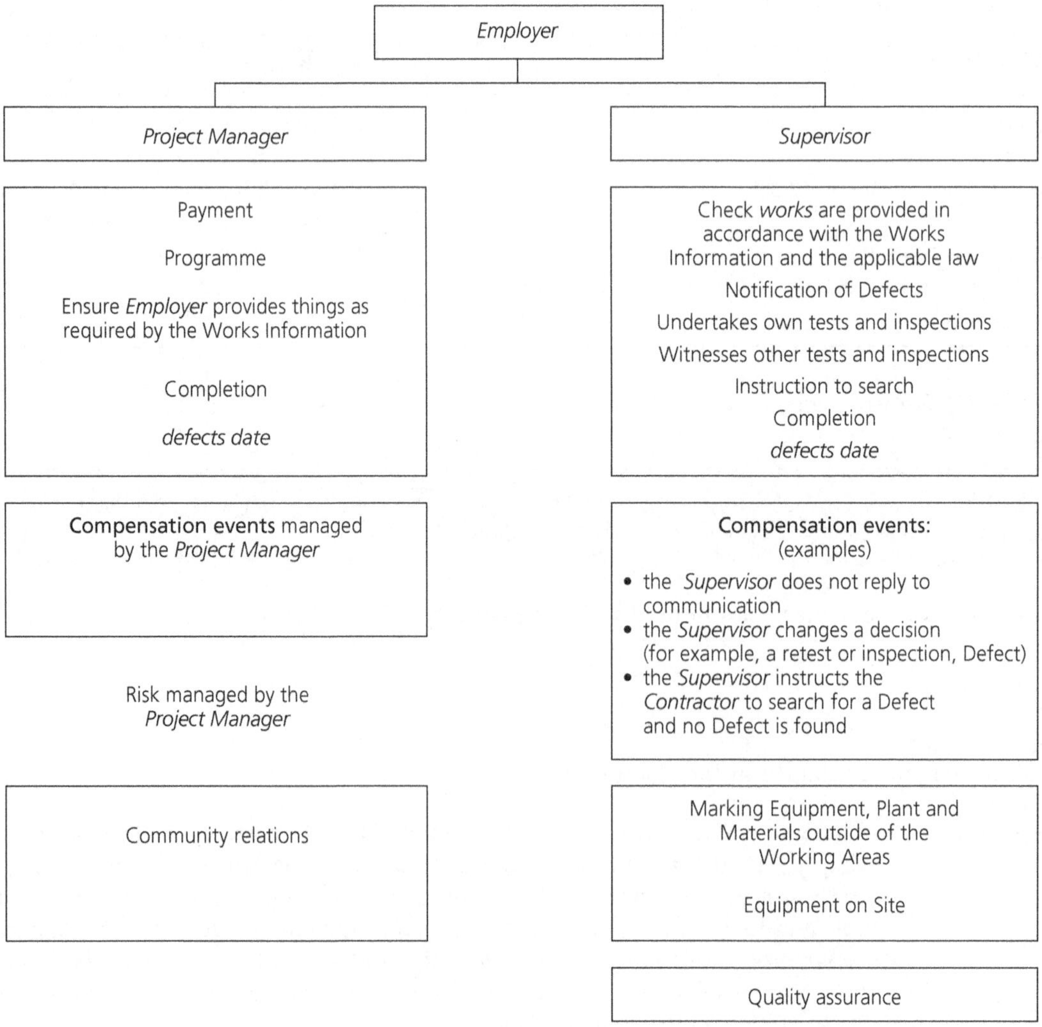

Comparison with other forms of contract

Table 1.4 outlines the named roles in the ECC and how they relate to similar roles in other forms of contract (with which those new to the ECC may be more familiar). The compared terms are not necessarily used in exactly the same way in all contracts and the roles do not necessarily carry out the same actions or have the same responsibilities.

Table 1.4 Comparison of contracts' terms

JCT	Other contracts	ECC
Employer	Employer	*Employer*
Architect	Engineer	*Project Manager*
Quantity Surveyor		
Clerk of Works	Engineer's Representative	***Supervisor***
	Site Agent/Inspector	
	Supervising Officer	
Adjudicator	Engineer (cl.66 decisions), Adjudicator/Conciliator	*Adjudicator*
Arbitrator	Arbitrator	*Tribunal,* for example, arbitrator or litigator

1.1.5   The *Supervisor* as part of the project team: project delivery systems

Section 1.1.4 identifies the roles within the ECC. There are other activities and responsibilities that these roles carry out; for example, the *Project Manager* carries out the commercial management of the contract as well as the role of designer or engineer. The *Project Manager* may choose to delegate these actions, such as to a quantity surveyor and an architect, but he is still ultimately responsible under the ECC.

Similarly, the *Supervisor* may delegate his actions to others. This is likely to happen on larger projects, where expertise is required across disciplines (e.g. building and mechanical/electrical). More specialised *Supervisor* roles may also be delegated, such as acoustic engineer or landscaper.

There are no formal rules about how to set up the organisation to deliver a project. How this is done will be influenced by many factors, such as:

- internal capability
- need for independence
- corporate governance requirements
- regulatory requirements
- multiple sponsors and
- assurance.

> **Key message**
>
> It is not just a question of filling in the boxes in Contract Data part one – you need to consider the political, governance and assurance issues for each of the named roles in the ECC.

Project delivery: the Supervisor *on a small project*
On small projects it is not unusual for the same person or organisation to be both *Project Manager* and *Supervisor.*

Project delivery: the Supervisor *on a large project*
The roles of *Project Manager* and *Supervisor* are most likely to be kept separate and independent, as envisaged by ECC.

Project delivery: the Supervisor *on a complex project*
For simple projects the *Supervisor* appointed by the *Employer* is likely to remain the same throughout. However, on more involved complex projects the *Employer* may have to consider the need to employ different *Supervisors* at different

Table 1.5 Typical project stages

Project stage	Description of stage
A	Design
B	Mobilisation
C	Off-site manufacture and fabrication ■ Prototypes
D	On-site construction ■ Building ■ Civils ■ Engineering services ■ IT ■ Process ■ Industrial systems
E	Testing and inspection/commissioning
F	Operational readiness
G	Safety case
H	Completion to the *defects date*

stages of the project and/or for the different disciplines (different organisations and different types of projects follow different project stages, for example, the RIBA Plan of Work, Association for Project Management – see Table 1.5).

Project delivery: the Supervisor *on a multi-*Employer *project*
Some projects may involve two or more sponsors. In some instances, one sponsor may be acting or appointed by a second sponsor as his agent for the delivery of the project. In such situations it is not uncommon for the party that is not actively engaged to want to assure his interests by having a separate and independent *Project Manager* and *Supervisor* for governance and assurance purposes. Sometimes the sponsor that is acting as the agent and has appointed the *Project Manager* and *Supervisor* may find himself at odds with the second sponsor, who may criticise the first for not managing the contract on his behalf effectively!

Quite clearly, in such situations, how the contractual management roles are organised, to whom they report and who should be appointed into those roles are matters of corporate governance and must be agreed between the sponsors at the outset of the project.

Key message

The fact that there is only one space for the name of the *Supervisor* should not deter you from entering more than one *Supervisor* for different stages of a project if it is appropriate.

Diagrams 1.5, 1.6 and 1.7 (Mitchell, B and Trebes, B (2012) *Managing Reality*, 2nd edn., Thomas Telford Publishing, London) (see Figures 1.5, 1.6 and 1.7) are examples of project models and are included here to show where the *Supervisor* may fit into the *Employer*'s project team (note that the health and safety role is often a separate role).

1.2.   Role of the *Supervisor*: overview of the *Supervisor* in the ECC
This section provides an overview of the role of the *Supervisor* to provide the frame for the detailed discussions in sections 3, 4 and 5.

1.2.1   Role of the *Supervisor*: clause 10.1
Clause 10.1 states that the *Supervisor* shall act as stated in the contract and in a spirit of mutual trust and co-operation.

Figure 1.5 The *Employer*'s team

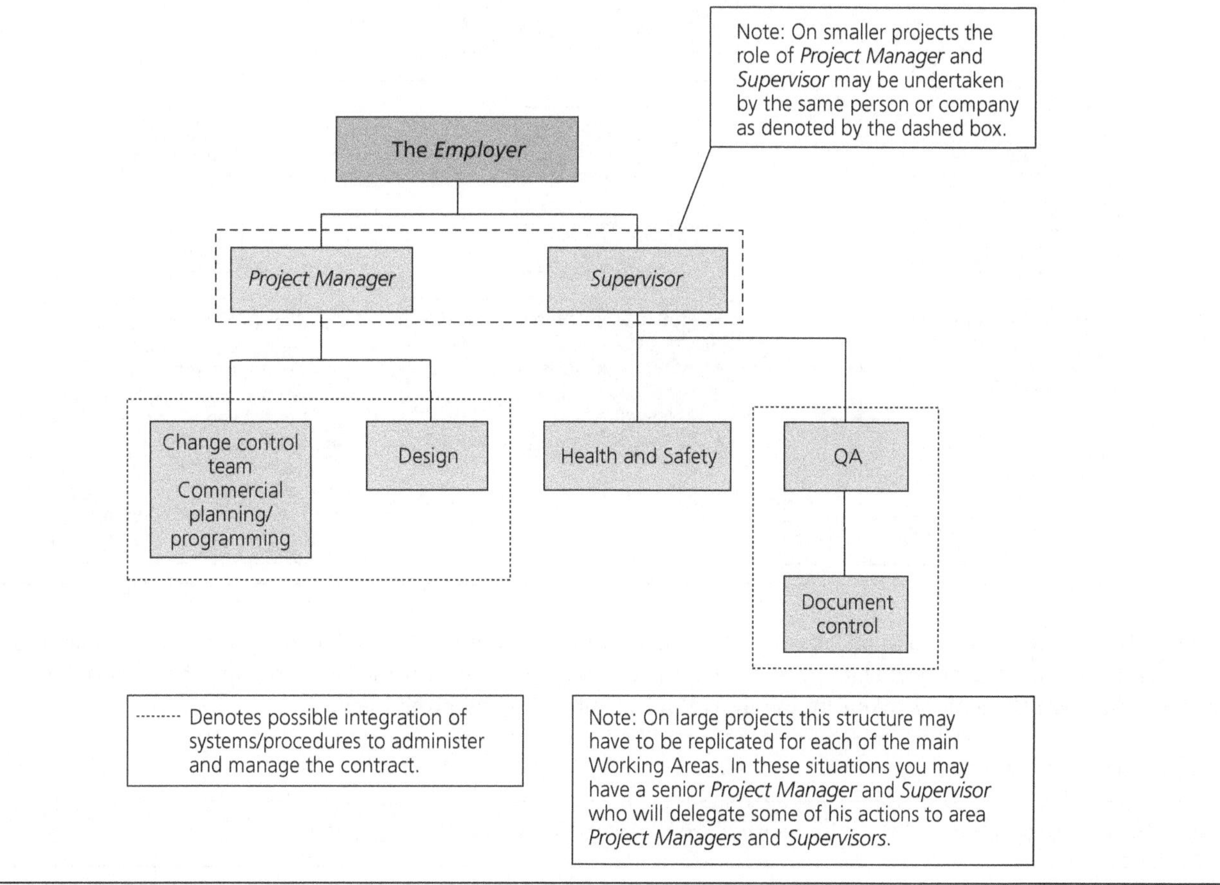

Figure 1.6 Integrated team 1

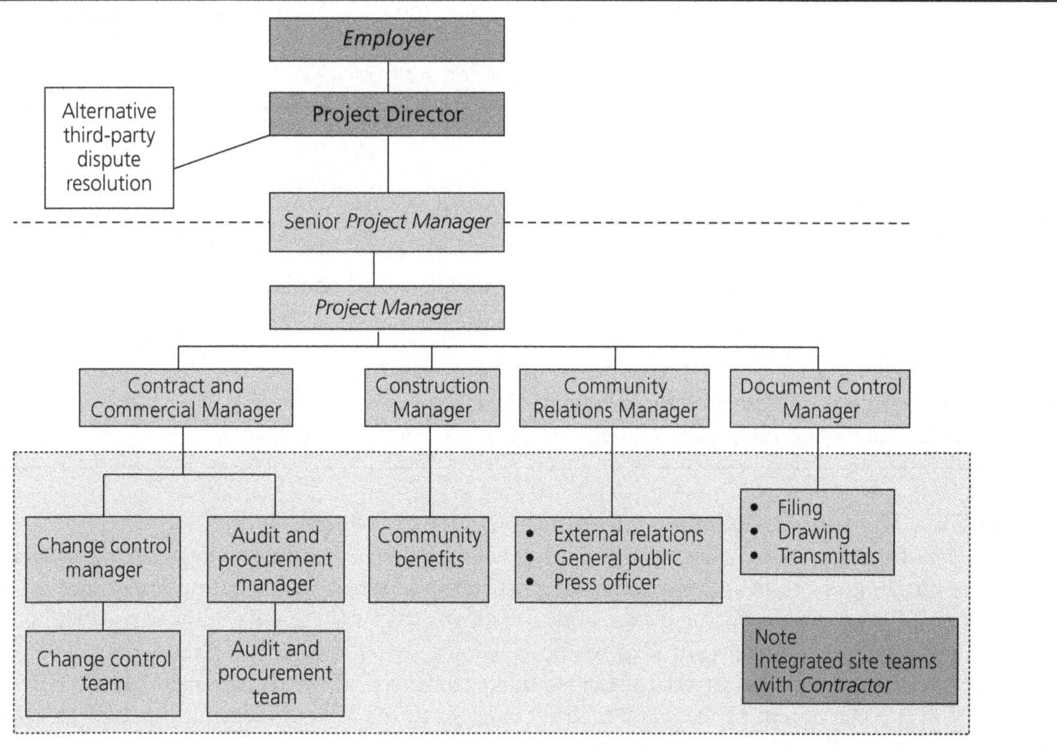

Figure 1.7 Integrated team 2

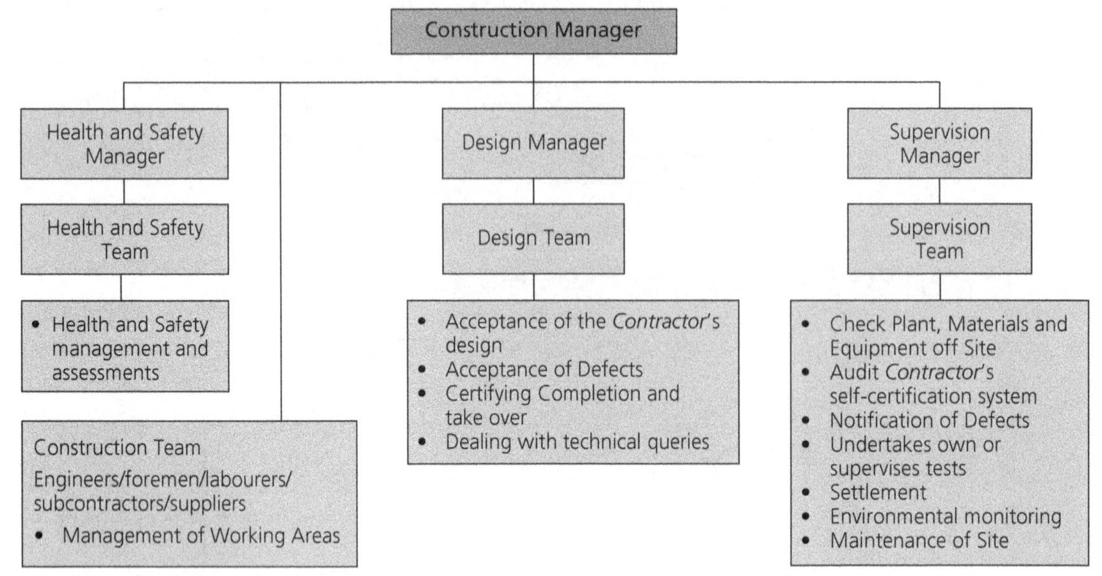

There have been endless discussions about 'mutual trust and co-operation' as well as numerous law articles and expert opinions. In the end, the project team must decide together what it means for their project, and the most obvious way to do this is through the actions taken by the individual members of the project team.

Act as stated in the contract

What does this mean?	It means do exactly what the contract states!

For example: comply with the timescales. Timescales are important, even if the timescales for the *Supervisor*'s actions are not as tightly defined as for the *Project Manager,* who has, for example, one week to respond to a notified compensation event:

- Comply with the *period for reply* (for all communications) – clause 13.3
- Do tests and inspections without causing unnecessary delay to the work – clause 40.5
- Issue the Defects Certificate at the later of the *defects date* and the end of the last *defect correction period* – clause 43.3
- Until the *defects date*, notify each Defect as soon as it is found – clause 42.2

Act in a spirit of mutual trust and co-operation

What does this mean?	It means behave in a trustworthy way and co-operate with others on the project team

For example: do what you say you will, when you say you will do it. Work together with the *Contractor* and others for the good of the project:

- Trust that the *Contractor* will notify Defects as he finds them – clause 42.2
- Work so as not to cause unnecessary delay – clause 40.5
- Work with the *Contractor* and the *Project Manager* to accept a Defect – clause 44.1

1.2.2 Role of the *Supervisor*: delineated from the *Project Manager*

The *Project Manager* does not abdicate his responsibility for the project outcome just because the *Supervisor* is involved in carrying out or watching the tests and inspections described in the Works Information and in notifying Defects. The *Project Manager* is still responsible for the *works*, and that means that it is the *Project Manager* who is responsible for the date of Completion, the final out-turn cost to the *Employer* and the quality of the *works*. The *Supervisor* must confine his actions to the scope of the services described in his contract and the requirements of the Works Information, but the *Project Manager* can accept Defects and instruct changes to the Works Information, and he is therefore just as actively involved in the quality of the *works* as the *Supervisor*.

> The *Supervisor* reports to the *Employer*, and works with the *Project Manager*.

The *Supervisor* is not required to report to the *Project Manager* in a direct line reporting manner and the *Supervisor* carries out his duties independently of the *Project Manager*. The *Employer* employs the *Supervisor*, and if there is any direct link or line management between these individuals in the organisation in which they work, it is not transferred to the operational procedures of the contract.

Of course, there is communication between the *Project Manager*, the *Employer* and the *Supervisor* – the contract would not work well if they did not talk to each other or worked in isolation. However, the relationships between these individuals are governed more by their professional contracts (whether internal, or through a professional contract such as the NEC3 Professional Services Contract) than by the ECC.

In some cases, the *Employer* may wish to have only one point of contact for a project, which will be the *Project Manager*. In other cases, the *Project Manager* may be concerned that he does not have sufficient control over the project and cannot manage the budget and programme if he cannot manage the quality of the project. In both these instances the *Supervisor* can undertake his actions through the *Project Manager*, the role of *Supervisor* is deleted and all *Supervisor* duties are performed by the *Project Manager*.

By acting as part of the team but working independently from the *Project Manager*, the *Supervisor* allows the *Project Manager* to concentrate on managing the project through administering the Risk Register and compensation events, enabling payment and monitoring progress through the programme. Where the *Supervisor* takes on the management of the notifying and correction of Defects, the *Project Manager* has more time to spend on moving the project forward positively, rather than being tied up monitoring the quality of the *works* and ensuring that they are being provided in accordance with the Works Information, logging Defects and discussing correction with the *Contractor*.

1.2.3   Role of the *Supervisor*: interactions of the *Supervisor*
The *Supervisor* interacts with all of the following people named in the contract:

- the *Employer*
- the *Contractor*
- the *Project Manager*
- the *Adjudicator* (named in the Contract Data; but interaction only takes place if a dispute is submitted for adjudication and the dispute involves the *Supervisor*).

Contractually, the *Supervisor* is required to interact with (inter alia) the *Contractor* and the *Project Manager*. However, there are many other people involved in the contract – that is, people other than the named parties in the Contract Data – with whom the *Supervisor* may be required to interact, or whom the *Supervisor* may come across at the Site. Examples are:

- anyone to whom the *Project Manager* has delegated actions, for example:
  - a quantity surveyor (payment)
  - a planner (the programme)
  - a risk analyser (the Risk Register)
  - an administrator (early warnings and compensation events)
- health and safety inspectors or specialists
- environmental inspectors or specialists
- building control officers
- community relations people
- insurance inspectors
- other *Supervisors* where the *Employer* requires expertise in several disciplines
- anyone on the design team for a design-and-build-style contract
- other officials, for example, planning
- utility providers
- Subcontractors and suppliers of Plant and Materials delivered to the Working Areas.

With the exception of the *Supervisor*'s duty to send his certificates to the *Project Manager* as well as the *Contractor* (clause 13.6), the ECC does not dictate the communications between the *Project Manager* and the *Supervisor*; the

Supervisor's actions are primarily related to communications with the *Contractor*. But, in reading the clauses, there can be no doubt that some communications between the *Supervisor* and the *Project Manager* will be required if the project is to be successful.

Example

The *Supervisor* carries out a test for airtightness of pipework. The *Employer* had to provide water for the test, and this is done in good time. But the result of the test is a fail and the *Supervisor* notifies the *Contractor* of the Defect.

The Defect notification is not a 'certificate' and therefore the *Supervisor* is not contractually required to notify the *Project Manager* of the test result. The Defect has to be corrected (still no contractual requirement to tell the *Project Manager*) and the test repeated. The *Contractor* tells the *Supervisor* in good time. But the things to be provided by the *Employer* (the water supply) are not ready and the test cannot go ahead, causing further delay to the programme. This time there is a valid compensation event and the *Contractor* could be entitled to an increase in the Prices and a delay to the Completion Date.

This example shows that the people involved in the contract cannot do their jobs in isolation. If the *Employer* is required to provide things for tests (supply water, power, specialist testing equipment, etc.), how does the *Employer* know when to provide them unless the *Supervisor* has communicated with the *Project Manager* or the *Employer* to ensure that they are on Site when needed for the test?

Figure 1.8 shows the people with whom the *Supervisor* will be required to interact as part of an ECC contract and others who may be working through the *Project Manager*, *Contractor* or *Employer*.

1.2.4   Role of the *Supervisor*: communications

The ECC requires the *Supervisor*'s communications to follow certain rules and these rules require professional record-keeping by the *Supervisor*. The *Supervisor* should liaise with the *Project Manager* to agree the format and frequency of communications, and likewise with the *Contractor*. In general, communications are more effective if a standard is created across the whole project. It is likely that the *Project Manager* will provide direction on the format and style of project communications.

The *Employer* should ensure that the relevant communications protocol is included in the scope of services for the *Project Manager* and the *Supervisor*, whether outsourced or not, and in the Works Information of the project so that all parties are using the same protocol.

The following lists the communication protocol required by the ECC.

1. All instructions, certificates and notifications (as well as other communications) from the *Supervisor* must be in a form which can be read, copied and recorded (clause 13.1).
2. All communications must be in the *language of the contract* (e.g. English) (clause 13.1).
3. The *Supervisor* must issue his certificates to the *Project Manager* and the *Contractor* (clause 13.6).
4. *Supervisor* notifications required by the contract must be communicated separately from other communications (clause 13.7).
5. The *Contractor* is required to obey an instruction provided by the *Supervisor* (clause 27.3) as long as it is in accordance with the contract.
6. Where the *Supervisor* is required to reply to a communication, he must do so within the *period for reply* (clause 13.3).

All of these communications can take place through a system set up by the *Employer* through the *Project Manager*, whether that is through particular software available on the market or through a simple database available to most computer users. Whatever method is chosen, it is recommended that a series of pro forma communications to be used on the project is set up, where each pro forma:

- has a unique identifier, for example, Project xxx/EW/001
- states the relevant clauses to which the communication relates
- refers to a timescale to facilitate timely communication by all parties
- contains a set distribution list, to facilitate contractually correct communication of notifications to all those expecting to receive them.

Figure 1.8 The breadth of communication that could be required of the *Supervisor*

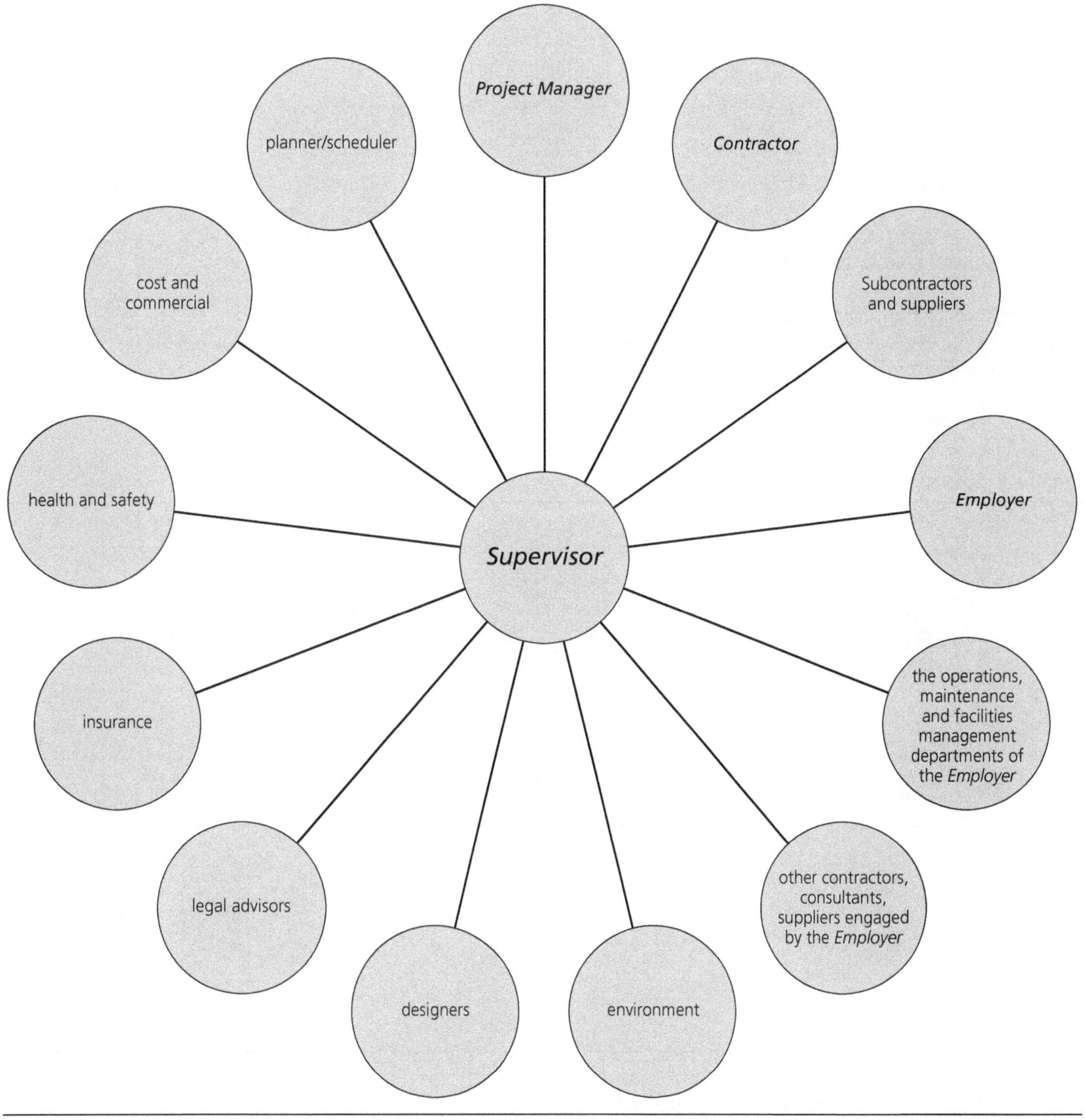

Appendix 5 includes a reference to and template forms for the communications that a *Supervisor* is contractually required to make.

Notifications required by the contract **must** be communicated separately from other communications. This means that every Defect must be notified separately from other communications to be made by the *Supervisor*.

Key message

Notifications required by the contract **must** be communicated separately from other communications.

Every Defect must be notified separately from other communications to be made by the *Supervisor*.

The *Contractor* and *Supervisor* must notify a Defect **'as soon as they find it'**.

The communications required from the *Supervisor* in an ECC contract relate to (refer also to section 3.3.3):

- delegation (clause 14.2)
- instructions (clause 27.3)
- test and inspection notification and results (clause 40.3)
- notification of Plant and Materials passing tests and inspections (clause 41.1)
- instruction to search (clause 42.1)
- Defect notification (clause 42.2)
- Defects Certificate (clause 43.3).

The *Supervisor* is required to take part in other communications and record other events, although these are not specifically mentioned in the ECC. Three examples are included here:

- vesting certificate to carry out the requirements of clause 70
- advising the *Project Manager* when Equipment, Plant and Materials have been marked for payment
- recording of events on Site and keeping a site diary.

Figure 1.9 shows the connectivity of Site communications .

Figure 1.9 Connectivity of Site communications

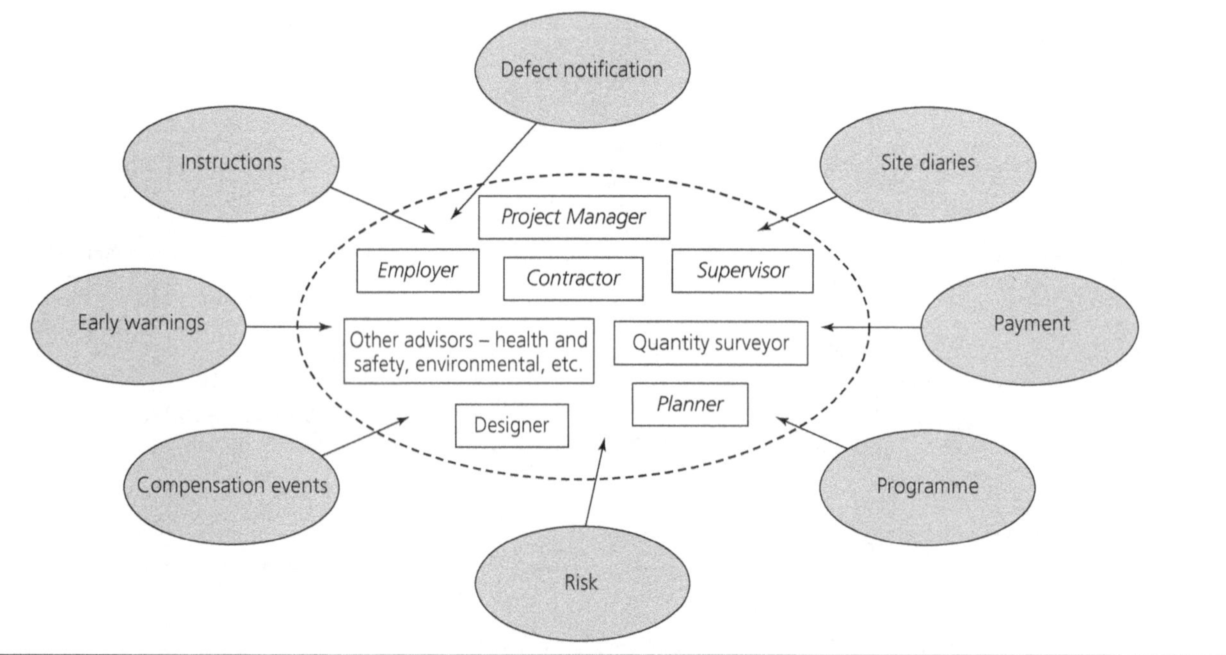

1.2.5   Role of the *Supervisor*: following the contract

Clause 10.1 requires the *Supervisor* to act as stated in the contract. There are consequences every time a person filling a contractual role in the ECC does not carry out that action or does not do so within the timescales set out in the contract. The ramifications may not be immediate or obvious, but, as with any other contract, all parties must work together to achieve the goal of the contract.

1.3.   Understanding the context: contract documents

As for any other named person in the contract, the requirements for the *Supervisor*'s actions are to be found in more than one document in the contract (Figure 1.10).

1.3.1   Main Options

When compiling the contract strategy for the project, the *Employer* can choose from six main Options and, in certain circumstances, can choose more than one main Option. The main Options determine how the *Contractor* will be paid for Providing the Works. The *Supervisor* is not contractually required to be a part of the decision-making team and the choice of main Option has very little impact on *Supervisor* actions, but they are listed here for the sake of completeness.

Figure 1.10 Sources of information: ECC contract documents

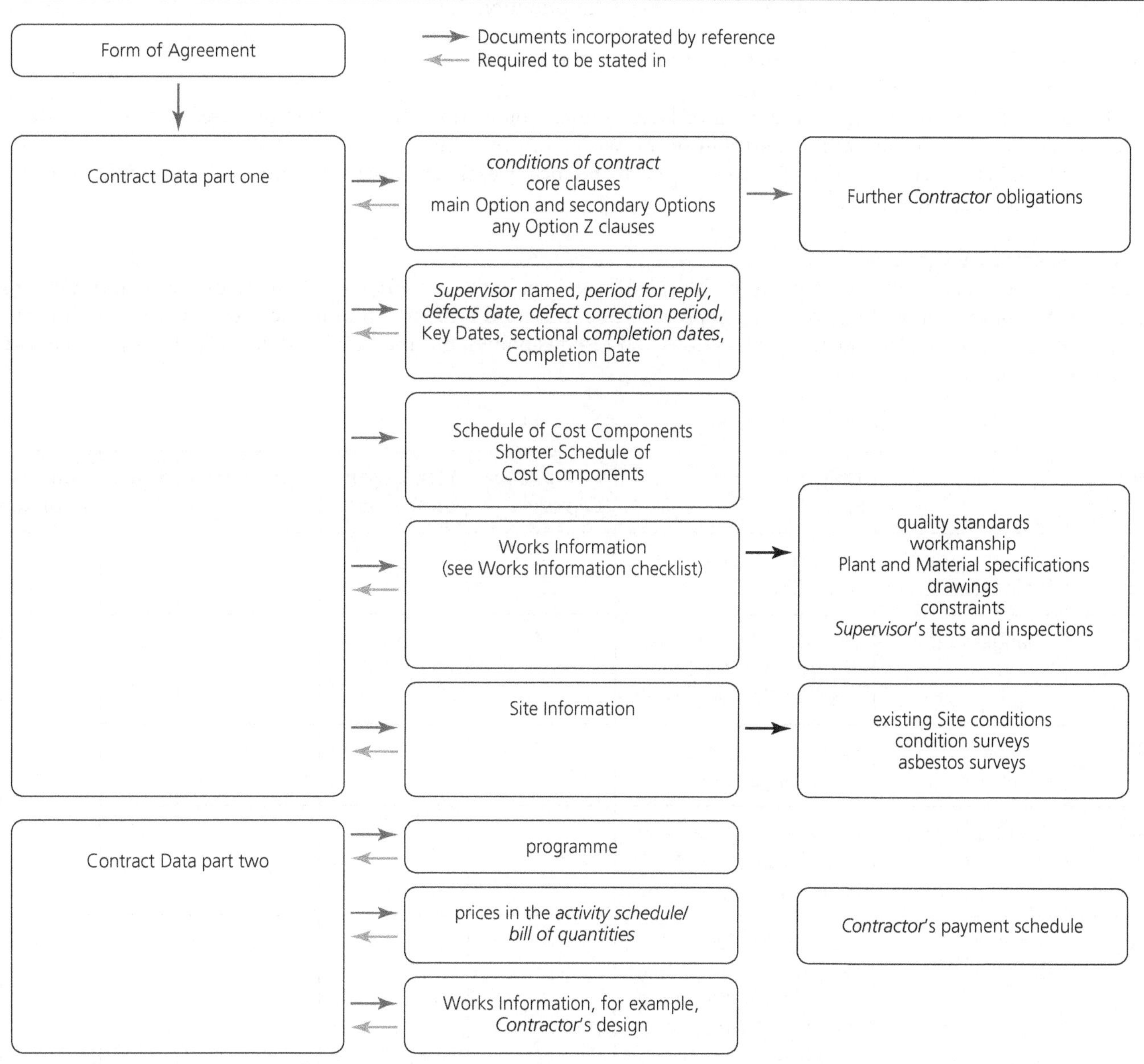

Main Option	Contract type
A – Priced contract with *activity schedule*	Lump sum contract
B – Priced contract with *bill of quantities*	*Remeasurement contract*
C – Target contract with *activity schedule*	Target contract with target established as a lump sum
D – Target contract with *bill of quantities*	Target contract with target established as a remeasurable sum
E – Cost reimbursable contract	Cost reimbursable contract
F – Management contract	Main *Contractor* is a management contractor who manages the work to be done and the work is broken down into work packages which are carried out by Subcontractors – *Employer* takes the risk of subcontract cost

The *Supervisor* can be an invaluable source of information for the *Project Manager* in assessing the amount due at each assessment date. For example, he will be able to provide information on:

- the use of Plant and Materials on Site (as recorded in the site diary)
- labour used (as recorded in the site diary)
- Disallowed Costs, for example, correction of Defects after Completion, or correction of a Defect caused by the *Contractor* not complying with a constraint in the Works Information
- costs of Defect correction, where this cost has been specifically excluded from the contract, for example, through the use of an Option Z clause.

1.3.2 Secondary Options

There are 19 secondary Options that can be included in the contract. The *Employer* will choose secondary Options based on the chosen contract strategy. The *Supervisor* does not need to be involved in the choice of Options, and the secondary Options have little impact on his actions and responsibilities, but they are listed here (Table 1.6) for the sake of completeness.

Table 1.6 ECC secondary Options

Ref	Option	Objective	Risk to the *Employer*	Risk to the *Contractor*	Commercial	Legal	Time related
X1	Price adjustment for inflation	*Employer* takes the risk of inflation	✓		✓		
X2	Changes in the law	*Employer* takes the risk of changes in the law after the Contract Date	✓			✓	
X3	Multiple currencies	*Employer* takes the risk of exchange rates	✓		✓		
X4	Parent company guarantee	Obtain a guarantee from the subsidiary's parent company		✓		✓	
X5	Sectional Completion	Requires the *Contractor* to complete part of the works in advance of the rest (X6 & X7 may be included)		✓	✓		✓
X6	Bonus for early Completion	Provides incentive to the *Contractor* for early Completion	✓		✓		✓
X7	Delay damages	Monies deducted if the *Contractor* is in delay (opposite of X6)		✓	✓		✓
X12	Partnering	Multi-partner agreement				✓	
X13	Performance bond	Performance bond imposed by the *Employer*			✓	✓	✓
X14	Advanced payment to the *Contractor*	Allows advanced payment to be made to the *Contractor*, for example, long lead-in items, pure advanced payment	✓		✓	✓	

Ref	Option	Objective	Risk to the *Employer*	Risk to the *Contractor*	Commercial	Legal	Time related
X15	Limitation of the *Contractor's* liability for his design to reasonable skill and care	If applied, this limits the *Contractor's* liability for his design down to reasonable skill and care	✓			✓	
X16	Retention	Retention deducted from the *Contractor*. This could be a percentage or a 'retention free amount'		✓	✓		
X17	Low performance damages	Monies deducted if performance standards are not achieved, for example, output of a power plant		✓	✓		
X18	Limitation of liability	This limits the overall liability of the *Contractor*	✓		✓	✓	
X20	Key Performance Indicators	Provides incentive to the *Contractor* as defined in the *incentive schedule*	✓		✓		✓
Y(UK)1	Project Bank Account	Allows the Parties and Subcontractors to manage the commercial elements of the project	✓		✓		
Y(UK)2	The Housing Grants, Construction and Regeneration Act 1996	Allows the *Employer* to stay within the law applicable to the payment on and adjudication for the project	✓		✓	✓	
Y(UK)3	The Contracts (Rights of Third Parties) Act 1999	Includes the Act where it is applicable.	✓		✓		
Z	*Additional conditions of contract*	Allows the *Employer* to allocate project risks.	✓	✓	✓	✓	

The *Employer* also has a choice of dispute resolution Options W1 and W2. The *Supervisor* does not need to be involved in the choice of dispute resolution Options, but the dispute resolution Option choice can impact on the *Supervisor* as follows.

- The *Supervisor* may be called upon to evidence activities on Site through providing copies of his site diaries.
- The *Supervisor* may be the cause of the dispute: 'an action of the *Supervisor* or the *Supervisor* not having taken an action'.

1.3.3 Core clauses

The *Supervisor* can find his primary actions and responsibilities in the core clauses and therefore he is required to be familiar with the core clauses, their impacts and the interactions required through them.

The core clauses are generic and contain standard procedures to be followed by all parties, including the *Supervisor*, and may be altered only through use of Option Z clauses for *additional conditions of contract*. The *Supervisor* should check to see if there are any Option Z clauses that may affect his role and responsibilities. The procedures described include:

- communication
- Defects management
- tests and inspections
- early warnings
- programme management
- compensation events.

Although the majority of the clauses affecting the *Supervisor* are contained within sections 4 and 7 of the core clauses, it is recommended that the *Supervisor* familiarises himself with all relevant core clauses, the main Option and the chosen secondary Options so that he understands the contract as a whole and also the wider impacts of his actions and responsibilities.

1.3.4   Contract Data

The Contract Data is the primary document in the contract as it embodies the contract strategy and refers to documents such as the Works Information and the pricing document, thereby including them into the contract. The Contract Data lists information relevant to the *Supervisor*, such as:

- the name and address of the *Supervisor* – Contract Data part one
- the *period for reply* – Contract Data part one
- the location of the Works Information – Contract Data part one
- the location of the Site Information – Contract Data part one
- the *defects date* – Contract Data part one
- the *defect correction period*, including any for different categories of Defects – Contract Data part one
- Works Information for the *Contractor*'s design – Contract Data part two
- the pricing document, for example, *activity schedule* or the *bill of quantities* – Contract Data part two
- the *boundaries of the site* – Contract Data part one
- the Site and Working Areas – Contract Data part two
- Option Z *additional conditions of contract*.

The *Supervisor* should be familiar with the Contract Data parts one and two and should understand the interaction between all of the documents within the contract.

1.3.5   Understanding key terms

Like any named party who is new to the ECC, the *Supervisor* should take time to familiarise himself with the documents that together comprise the contract, and with the rules and procedures within them. In this section, some of the protocols used within the ECC as relevant to the *Supervisor* are described.

In general, an ECC contract will comprise the following.

- Form of agreement – this may be a simple 'letter of award' or 'acceptance letter', but it would preferably be a two- or three-page form of agreement/contract that outlines the rights and obligations of the parties and is signed by both the *Employer* and the *Contractor*.
- Contract Data part one – completed by the *Employer*.
- Contract Data part two – completed by the *Contractor*.
- All documents included in the Contract Data parts one and two by reference, for example:
  - core clauses
  - a main Option
  - secondary Options
  - Works Information by the *Employer,* including, for example, health and safety information
  - Works Information by the *Contractor,* including, for example, the *Contractor*'s design
  - Site Information
  - the pricing document, such as an *activity schedule* or a *bill of quantities*
  - a programme – Contract Data part two (unless Contract Data part one states it should be produced post-award).

All these documents together make up the contract strategy – the project team will have decided that each is required as it forms an element of the strategy for that project. For example, the contract may include for:

■ remeasurable payment (main Option B), where the *Contractor* tenders a total of the Prices but is paid for the actual quantity of work he undertakes
■ delay damages (secondary Option X7), where a delay in the completion of the project will have an adverse effect on the *Employer*, for example, lost rent or revenue in the case of a retail building
■ sectional Completion (secondary Option X5), where the *Employer* wishes to use some parts of the *works* before other parts.

The following drafting principles are used in the ECC.

■ Terms in *italics* are project specific and are identified in the Contract Data, for example, *period for reply* and *completion date*.
■ Defined terms have capital initials and are defined in clause 11.2, for example, Defect, Completion, Works Information.
■ The definitions in clause 11.2 may refer the user directly to the Contract Data for project-specific information, for example, 'The Completion Date is the *completion date*'.
■ Additional defined terms and identified terms may be relevant depending on which main Option and secondary Options are chosen, for example, the Price for Work Done to Date, *section* of the *works*.

1.3.6   Some defined terms and basic linkages within the contract

There are no cross-references between clauses in the ECC. One result of this is that links between clauses may not be immediately obvious.

For example, one of the critical clauses for the *Supervisor* refers to the notification of Defects. Clause 42.2 provides: 'Until the *defects date*, the *Supervisor* notifies the *Contractor* of each Defect as soon as he finds it and the *Contractor* notifies the *Supervisor* of each Defect as soon as he finds it.' There is an obvious referral to clause 11.2(5) for the definition of a Defect, but there are other links to the correction of Defects in clauses 43.1 and 43.2.

The *Supervisor* needs to understand how his actions are linked to both the actions of others and to other actions of his own. Table 1.7 lists some of the defined terms and basic linkages within the ECC.

> The index by clause number at the back of the ECC can be used as a quick reference guide for key words used in the contract. It also identifies associated clauses. For example, on page 82:
>
> Defect(s)
>   notifying 11.2(6), 42.2, 43.1–2

1.3.7   The Accepted Programme

The programme by which the ECC project is governed is submitted by the *Contractor* to the *Project Manager*. It will be submitted either with the tender or within a specified time (stated in weeks) after contract award, and then at the intervals as stated in the Contract Data. The programme should be detailed – for example, it should include a list of resources for activities so that it can be used to forecast the cost of any change. Once accepted by the *Project Manager*, the programme becomes the Accepted Programme (defined in clause 11.2(1)) and it can be used by other people, including the *Supervisor*, to help them understand how their role affects or is affected by the project's programme.

Clause 31.2 lists the dates and other information that must be included on the programmes submitted by the *Contractor* to the *Project Manager* for acceptance. The programme information listed in Table 1.8 will be pertinent to the *Supervisor*.

1.3.8   The Works Information

Works Information is a defined term (clause 11.2(19)). It is also mentioned in both Contract Data part one and Contract Data part two. It is referred to throughout the core clauses, is used constantly by all the key people on the project and is arguably the most important part of the contract, certainly for the *Supervisor*.

> **Key message**
>
> Any change to the Works Information is a compensation event – no matter how small the change.

Table 1.7 Basic linkages within the ECC

Clause	Defined term and comment	Linkage
11.2(2)	**Completion** General – the second bullet serves as a basic filter, the first bullet allows the *Employer* to be very precise Bullet one refers to the Works Information and the Completion Date Bullet two refers to Defects and Others	Works Information – the *Employer* should ensure that the Works Information details what needs to be done before the Completion Date 20.1 – it is the *Contractor*'s responsibility to make sure that he adheres to the Works Information 30.1 – it is the *Contractor*'s responsibility to complete the *works* before the Completion Date 42.2 – the *Contractor* and the *Supervisor* both notify Defects 43.1 and 43.2 – detail when the *Contractor* should correct Defects 30.2 – it is the *Project Manager* who decides when Completion has been reached
11.2(5)	**Defect** Bullet one relates to the Works Information Bullet two relates to applicable law and accepted design The clause relates to the *Project Manager*, the *Contractor*, the *Supervisor* and the Works Information	20.1 – it is the *Contractor*'s responsibility to make sure that he adheres to the Works Information, that is, both Works Information by the *Employer* and Works Information by the *Contractor* for his design 42.2 – the *Contractor* and the *Supervisor* both notify Defects 43.1 and 43.2 – detail when the *Contractor* should correct Defects 44.1 – allows the *Project Manager* to accept a Defect 45.2 – refers to Defects for which access is required 11.2(22) or (23) or (24) – Defined Cost excludes the cost of Defects in certain circumstances
11.2(6)	**Defects Certificate** Refers to Defects, the *Supervisor* and the *defects date*	43.3 – describes when the *Supervisor* issues the Defects Certificate 45.1 – describes the process of other people correcting the Defect if the *Contractor* does not correct it as required
11.2(10)	**Others** For example, local authorities, archaeologist	60.1(5) The *Employer* and Others work within the times shown on the Accepted Programme Used in 11.2(2) definition of Completion
11.2(18)	**Working Areas** Necessary for Providing the Works and used only for work on this contract	15.1 – adding to the Working Areas 70.1 – *Employer's* title to Plant and Materials 71.1 – marking Equipment, Plant and Materials outside the Working Areas Schedule of Cost Components – resources within the Working Areas
11.2(19)	**Works Information** Specifies and describes the *works* or any constraints	11.2(2) – definition of Completion 11.2(5) – definition of a Defect 40.1 – tests and inspections 45 – uncorrected Defects

Table 1.8 The Accepted Programme

Programme detail	Useful to the *Supervisor*
Dates: *starting date*, *access dates*, Key Dates, Completion Date	All dates will aid the *Supervisor*'s understanding of where his duties will slot into the programme. Of particular use to the *Supervisor* is the Completion Date and the *defects date* as both these dates are dependent upon the correction of Defects. Even though it is the *Project Manager* who decides the date of Completion, reaching Completion depends on the correction of Defects that would stop the *Employer* or Others using the *works* and therefore the *Supervisor* should be consulted by the *Project Manager* prior to his decision to issue the Completion certificate.
The order and timing of operations and work by Others	The *Supervisor* can work out when he will be required to carry out tests/inspections and when to make sure that materials needed for tests/inspections are available. These details will also aid the *Supervisor*'s understanding of how the *Contractor* plans to progress the *works* so that the *Supervisor* can be present at the Site for record/site diary purposes.
For each operation a statement of how the *Contractor* plans to do the work, identifying principal Equipment and resources	These will help the *Supervisor* understand how the *Contractor* intends to carry out tests/inspections and also what resources he needs so that the *Supervisor* can note these for record/site diary purposes.
Provisions for health and safety requirements	The *Supervisor* may be required to check on the *Contractor*'s quality management system, which may include the health and safety measures used by the *Contractor*.
When the *Contractor* will take delivery of and then use Equipment, Plant and Materials that the *Supervisor* is required to mark	The *Supervisor* may be required to mark Equipment, Plant and Materials before delivery, or they may need to be tested or inspected before delivery.
When *Contractor* tests and inspections will take place and when the *Contractor* needs the materials to carry out the test	This will advise the *Supervisor* of when tests and inspections by the *Contractor* are planned to take place so that he may witness them.
Information that the Works Information requires the *Contractor* to show	This information could include: ■ the order and timing of when things will be needed by the *Employer* ■ procedures, for example, those required for the purposes of title (section 7 of the core clauses) ■ *Supervisor* activities: key dates for the inspection of the *Contractor*'s work to check for Defects; dates when he may be required to mark Plant and Materials outside the Working Areas; dates when he may be required to mark Equipment ■ dates for tests/inspections by the *Supervisor*.

What is the Works Information?

Before looking at how to write the Works Information (www.neccontract.com, *How to Write the ECC Works Information*, 2013, Thomas Telford, London), the following list outlines, in broad terms, what to look for in the Works Information:

- a specification for the *works*
- a description of the *works*
- constraints on how the *works* can be provided
- information about what the *Contractor* is to design
- a description of things to be included in each programme submitted by the *Contractor*
- descriptions of tests and inspections to be carried out during the *works* by the *Contractor* and *Supervisor*
- the standards against which Defects are to be judged on an objective basis
- facilities, materials and samples to be provided, and any conditions affecting how the work is to be done
- how and when to mark Equipment, Plant and Materials that are outside the Working Areas.

The Works Information is critical because any change to the Works Information is a compensation event. While not all changes will increase the Prices or delay the Completion Date, the *Employer*, the *Project Manager* and the *Supervisor* must understand that any instructions that contradict the Works Information could potentially affect the results of the project. A change in the Works Information could be a result of:

- illegal or impossible requirements (clause 18.1)
- ambiguity or contradiction within the Works Information (clause 17.1) or between the Works Information and another contract document, for example, Site Information or Contract Data
- missing information, for example, no specification for concrete works (clause 60.1(1))
- under- or over-specification
- work that was incompletely specified at the start of the contract.

Where is the Works Information?

The Works Information provided by the *Employer* can be found in the documents that the Contract Data part one states it is in. If it is Works Information for the *Contractor*'s design, it can be found in the documents that the Contract Data part two states it is in.

Why does the *Supervisor* need the Works Information?

The *Supervisor* must refer to the Works Information all the time to do his job: he will need it to compare the *works* with the Works Information and to carry out and watch tests and inspections. Even if the *Supervisor* does not draft the Works Information, he needs to understand and be comfortable with the Works Information and believe it is as complete as possible.

Key message

The Works Information provides an objective test of what is and what is not a Defect in an ECC project.

Frequently asked questions

The contract includes two sets of Works Information: Works Information provided by the *Employer* and (for *Contractor* designed *works*) Works Information provided by the *Contractor* and submitted as part of his tender. Which one takes precedence?	If a change to the Works Information provided by the *Contractor* for his design is made at his request or to comply with other Works Information provided by the *Employer*, it is **not** a compensation event (clause 60.1(1) bullet two). In that respect, the Works Information provided by the *Employer* takes precedence over the Works Information provided by the *Contractor* for his design.

What if there are inconsistencies between the Works Information that the *Contractor* provides (for his design) as part of his tender and the Works Information that he submits later, during the period of the contract?	The *Contractor*'s primary obligation is to Provide the Works in accordance with the Works Information (clause 20.1). If there are inconsistencies between sets of information provided by the *Contractor*, the *Project Manager* gives an instruction resolving the ambiguity or inconsistency (clause 17.1). A change to the Works Information provided by the *Contractor* for his design that is made at his request or to comply with other Works Information provided by the *Employer* is **not** a compensation event (clause 60.1(1) bullet two).
Where does the *Supervisor* look to find out if work contains a Defect?	■ In the Works Information provided by the *Employer* referred to in Contract Data part one. ■ In the Works Information provided by the *Contractor* referred to in Contract Data part two. ■ In any instructions given by the *Project Manager*. ■ In any changes to the Works Information made since the start of the contract. ■ In legislation, regulations and guidance referenced in the Works Information. ■ In legislation not referenced in the Works Information but nevertheless applicable to the *works*. ■ *Contractor* design which the *Project Manager* has accepted.
Can the *Supervisor* instruct a change to the Works Information?	Only the *Project Manager* has the authority to change the Works Information (clause 14.3). If the *Supervisor* thinks something is incorrect, he should not instruct the change, but should tell the *Project Manager*. However, the *Contractor* must obey an instruction given by the *Supervisor* that is given in accordance with the contract (clause 27.3). There is no restitution for a *Contractor* who obeys an instruction of the *Supervisor* that is other than an instruction to search.

Key message

Only the *Project Manager* has the authority to issue an instruction that changes the Works Information (clause 14.3).

If the *Supervisor* thinks that something the *Contractor* is doing is wrong but the *Contractor* is following the Works Information then the *Supervisor* should advise the *Project Manager*, who can then issue an instruction as required to change the Works Information.

Errors in the Works Information provided by the *Employer* are not Defects for which the *Contractor* is liable.

Section 2

NEC3: The Role of the *Supervisor*
ISBN 978-0-7277-6096-8

Supervisor duties

2.1. Context: the *Supervisor*'s responsibilities

2.1.1 Introduction

When asked what the *Supervisor* does, many people would say that the *Supervisor* is responsible for the quality of the *works*. This is partly true, and is heavily qualified, as will become apparent in this book.

The *Supervisor* cannot be equated directly with a traditional clerk of works; although elements of the two roles are the same, in the ECC, the *Supervisor* is independent of the other contractual roles, including the *Project Manager*.

> **Key message**
>
> *Supervisor* ≠ clerk of works

For the purposes of this book, there are two sets of duties that can be carried out by the *Supervisor*:

- the *Supervisor*'s actions required by the ECC
- actions through which the *Supervisor* can bring added value to the project.

The glossary of terms in Appendix 7B of this book will aid understanding of the *Supervisor*'s role.

2.1.2 Beyond the ECC

The *Supervisor*:

- tests and inspects the *works* for compliance with the Works Information
- manages the Defects process
- checks Equipment, Plant and Materials and marks them to protect the *Employer*'s interests.

The *Supervisor* is responsible only for the quality of the work and tests and inspections required by the Works Information or the applicable law, as indicated by the following.

- A Defect is defined as work that is not in accordance with the **Works Information** (clause 11.2 (5)).
- The *Contractor* and the *Supervisor* carry out tests in accordance with the **Works Information** and the applicable law (clause 40.1).

> **Key message**
>
> The *Supervisor* is responsible only for the quality of the work and tests and inspections **required by the Works Information** or the applicable law.

Most of the focus in the ECC is on the *Project Manager*, but the *Supervisor* may well be on Site more frequently than the *Project Manager*. It is also likely that the *Project Manager* will trust the *Supervisor* to report on matters that go beyond the boundaries of the ECC. For example:

- It is likely that the *Supervisor* will meet regularly with the *Project Manager* to discuss:
  - Defects
  - progress on Site
  - events or matters of concern, for example, the quality of the *Contractor*'s and his Subcontractors' work.
- It is unlikely that the *Project Manager* will make a decision about accepting a Defect without consulting the *Supervisor* and other members of the team, such as the designer.

The *Supervisor* must therefore be sufficiently experienced and knowledgeable to understand the *works* and be able to identify when things are not proceeding according to the requirements of the project.

However, these interactions are not part of the ECC and the *Employer* may choose to include his expectations in the contract with the *Supervisor* and include some elements of the *Contractor–Supervisor* relationship in the Works Information.

> **Key message**
>
> The *Supervisor* can help to support the management and delivery of the *works* and support the *Employer*'s team by keeping records and acting as their **eyes and ears on the Site**.

The *Supervisor* is only responsible for health and safety reporting or inspections where the health and safety information is included in the Works Information and the law and it impacts on the *works* in comparison to the Works Information.

2.2. *Supervisor* responsibilities required by the ECC

Guidelines on the *Supervisor*'s communications are included in section 1.2.4 – the *Supervisor* must follow these rules to be in compliance with the ECC.

A *Supervisor* should also understand that:

- the *Supervisor* can cause a compensation event by:
  - giving an instruction or issuing a certificate (clause 61.1)
  - not replying to a communication from the *Contractor* within the period required by the contract (clause 60.1(6))
  - changing a decision which he has previously communicated to the *Contractor* (clause 60.1(8))
  - instructing the *Contractor* to search for a Defect and no Defect is found, unless the search is needed **only because** the *Contractor* gave insufficient notice of doing work obstructing a required test or inspection (clause 60.1(10) – see Appendix 1 for further information on the consequences of this clause)
  - causing unnecessary delay when doing a test or inspection (clause 60.1(11))
- no action of the *Supervisor* will result in termination rights
- the *Adjudicator* can revise any action or inaction of the *Supervisor* (Option clause W1.3(5) and W2.3(4) – action or inaction of the *Supervisor*).

> **Key message**
>
> The *Supervisor* must liaise with the *Project Manager* about Defects, tests and inspections.

There are also other duties and actions under the contract that the *Supervisor* needs to recognise, but which have little direct impact:

- The *Supervisor* must first notify the *Contractor* before delegating or cancelling the delegation of any of his actions (see Appendix 5A and 5B for forms to be used for delegation) (clause 14.2).
- The *Supervisor*'s acceptance of a communication from the *Contractor* does not change the *Contractor*'s responsibility to Provide the Works or his liability for his design (clause 14.1).
- The *Supervisor*'s acceptance of the *Contractor*'s work does not change the *Contractor*'s responsibility to Provide the Works or his liability for his design (clause 14.1).
- The *Supervisor* may be instructed by the *Contractor* or the *Project Manager* to attend a risk reduction meeting to discuss an early warning (clause 16.2).

All of this information is provided with the knowledge that the *Supervisor* has relatively few express actions under the ECC. Examples of these actions are as follows.

- There is only one instruction that the ECC expressly allows the *Supervisor* to make – to search for a Defect.
- There is only one certificate that the *Supervisor* is expressly required to provide – the Defects Certificate.
- The ECC does not expressly require the *Supervisor* to provide assumptions and therefore there will be no need for him to correct them (correction leads to a compensation event (clause 61.1)).
- The ECC does not expressly require the *Contractor* to send the *Supervisor* a communication to which the *Supervisor* is required to reply (an untimely reply leads to a compensation event (clause 60.1(6)).
- The ECC does not expressly provide reasons under which the *Supervisor* may accept or not accept a communication from the *Contractor* (use of a reason not listed in the contract leads to a compensation event under clause 60.1(9)).
- The ECC does not specifically mention a decision that the *Supervisor* is required to communicate to the *Contractor* (changing a previously communicated decision leads to a compensation event under clause 60.1(8)).

The Works Information should set out the tests and inspections to be undertaken by the *Contractor* and *Supervisor*.

> **Key message**
>
> The *Contractor* has a contractual obligation to Provide the Works in accordance with the Works Information (clause 20.1) and is 100% responsible for this being fulfilled.
>
> The *Supervisor* is there to ensure as best he can that the *works* provided by the *Contractor* are constructed in accordance with the Works Information and the applicable law.
>
> The *Supervisor*'s acceptance of a *Contractor*'s communication or of his design does not change the *Contractor*'s responsibility to Provide the Works or his liability for his design (clause 14.1).

2.2.1   Contractor self-certification of quality

Some contracts contain a requirement in the Works Information for the *Contractor* to operate a quality self-certification system in which they supervise and are responsible for the management of the quality of the *works*. In such situations it may be interpreted that the *Contractor* is essentially fulfilling the role and actions of the *Supervisor*.

In these situations the *Employer*'s management team take on a quality management surveillance role in which they audit and monitor the *Contractor*'s self-certification system to ensure that it is being operated and followed. The *Employer* will include within the *conditions of contract* and other contract documentation safeguards, sanctions and remedies to protect his interests. The following are given as examples.

- The *Contractor* submits his quality control self-certification proposals as part of his tender submission.
- The *Contractor* submits his self-certification quality control system for acceptance by the *Project Manager* within four weeks of the Contract Date. The *Contractor* updates and maintains his quality system at regular intervals while Providing the Works.
- The *Employer*'s team monitor the *Contractor*'s self-certification quality control system to check that it is being applied correctly and undertake spot checks during the contract period and when parts of the *works* are finished.
- On main Options C, D and E contracts, the *Contractor* is incentivised to manage and apply his quality control self-certification system correctly as Defects identified by the *Contractor* are paid as part of his actual Defined Cost. If Defects are not notified but are picked up by the *Employer*'s quality control audit and monitoring team then these are not allowed and not paid by the *Employer*.
- The *Contractor*'s failure to follow his own quality self-certification system or quality management system may be notified as a Defect.
- Remedying Defects that arise because the *Contractor* did not follow his self-certification or quality management system is a Disallowed Cost.
- The persistent failure to follow his own system or a failure to remedy a non-conformance or failure in his system notified by the *Project Manager* within an identified time period could lead to the termination of the contract, or to the application of step-in rights that allow the *Employer* to appoint his own *Supervisor* or system and to recover the costs from payments due to the *Contractor*.
- Use of Key Performance Indicators for the demonstration of the achievement of quality objectives and targets (ECC secondary Option X20).
- A requirement for the *Contractor* to identify in Contract Data part two his key people and to list their qualifications and experience, for example, membership of a recognised body, qualifications as a quality professional, competency as a quality auditor, knowledge and experience of developing quality management systems.

2.2.2 *Contractor's* quality management system

Most contractors operate a BS EN ISO 9001: 2008 (ISO 9001)-style quality management system (QMS). ISO 9001 talks about 'non-conformance': a non-conformance means that something has gone wrong – a problem has occurred and needs to be addressed. A non-conformance is addressed with corrective actions. ISO 9001 requires documentation of the non-conformance procedure and the keeping of records of non-conformance issues identified and actions taken.

However, the operation of an ISO 9001 QMS and the recording of non-conformances is not the same as giving the required notification of a Defect as required by ECC clause 42.2. The correct notification of Defects is important to protect the *Employer*'s interests in relation to uncorrected Defects (clause 45), accepting Defects (clause 44) and for the issue of the Defects Certificate (clause 43.3).

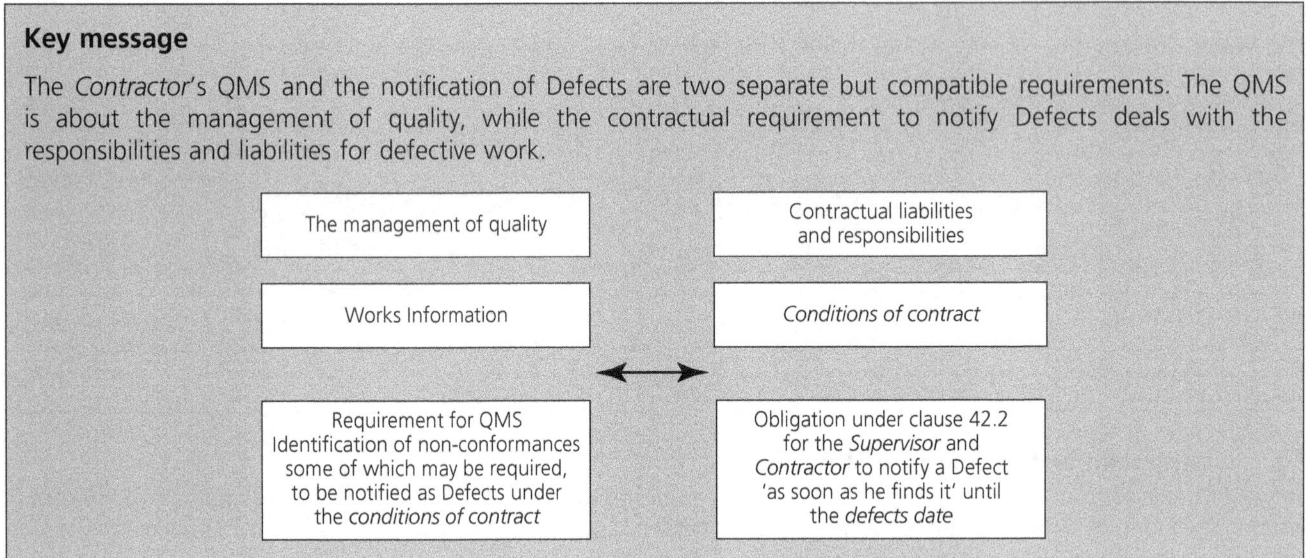

The following lists the *Supervisor* actions that may trigger a compensation event.

1. Issuing a certificate to the *Contractor* (and to the *Project Manager*)

Clause 43.3	The *Supervisor* **must** issue the Defects Certificate.
	■ Clause 13.6 advises the recipients as the *Contractor* and the *Project Manager*.
	■ Clause 11.2(6) provides the definition of the Defects Certificate.
	■ The following clauses are influenced by the Defects Certificate:
	  – clause 50.1, payment
	  – clauses 80.1, 81.1, 82.1, risks
	  – clause 84.2, insurance
	  – clause X16.2, retention
	  – clause X17.1, low performance damages
	  – clause X18.3, liability limitation
	  – clause X20.2, KPIs.

2. Issuing a notification

Clause 40.3	The *Supervisor* **must** notify the *Contractor* of his [the *Supervisor's*] tests and inspections before they start.
Clause 40.3	The *Supervisor* **must** notify the *Contractor* of the results of his [the *Supervisor's*] tests and inspections.
Clause 41.1	The *Supervisor* **must** notify the *Contractor* if Plant and Materials have passed the test or inspection.
Clause 42.2	The *Supervisor* **must** notify the *Contractor* of each Defect as defined in clause 11.2(5).

3. Issuing an instruction

Clause 42.1	The *Supervisor* **may** instruct the *Contractor* to search.

4. Replying to a communication from the *Contractor*

Clause 40.3	The *Supervisor* **may** receive notification from the *Contractor* that he [the *Contractor*] is going to carry out a test or inspection (but no reply is required).
Clause 40.3	The *Supervisor* **may** receive notification from the *Contractor* of the results of his [the *Contractor's*] test or inspection (but no reply is required).

The ECC does not expressly require the *Supervisor* to reply to a communication from the *Contractor*.

5. Communicating a decision

The ECC does not require the *Supervisor* to communicate any decisions to the *Contractor* (the providing of a Defect notification implies a decision but is covered under the issuing of a notification, which is treated differently from the communication of a decision).

6. Carrying out a test or inspection or watching any test

Clause 40.5	The *Supervisor* does his tests and inspections without causing unnecessary delay to the work or to a payment which is conditional upon a test or inspection being successful.
Clause 40.3	The *Supervisor* may watch any test done by the *Contractor*.

For a full list of the *Supervisor*'s actions see Appendix 1.

2.3. *Supervisor* duties not explicitly required by the ECC

The *Supervisor* cannot work in isolation. Although he has few express actions and duties in comparison with the *Project Manager*, he is likely to be involved in most of the major events that take place during the contract, such as compensation events, payment, the programme, Defects, Disallowed Cost and disputes.

The *Project Manager*'s job will be harder if the *Supervisor* does not communicate with the *Project Manager* as much as he could. A lack of interaction could lead to the *Project Manager* being unaware of events managed by the *Supervisor* occurring on the Site that could impact on the cost, time or quality of the project.

Appendix 1 describes the ECC clauses that impact directly on the *Supervisor* and the ECC clauses which are peripheral to the *Supervisor*'s duties but which affect the way he interacts with the *Project Manager* and others.

2.3.1 Overview of the *Supervisor's* involvement in the project

*Supervisor*s are often not involved or appointed on a project until it starts on Site; however, there is no doubt that the *Supervisor* can be of use to the project team far earlier in a project life cycle. The following are the stages of a project to which the *Supervisor* can contribute.

1	Business decision to procure the *works* project
2	Compilation of documentation to be issued with the invitation to tender, for example, Works Information specifications
3	Evaluation of tenders to determine the best value for money in accordance with the evaluation criteria
4	Decisions on what documents/concepts are included in the contract
5	Recording of site condition survey, for example, photos of fences, pavements, access routes

6	Start-up meeting
7	Pre-construction (if any)
8	During construction
9	Post-construction
10	Project close out

A professional joining a project part way through to act as the *Supervisor* will need to take stock of the project and consider what to look for, how to approach the role, what systems to put in place, etc.

> **Key message**
>
> As one experienced project manager once said, *'It is not a crime to be over cost or behind programme. It is a crime, however, not to know that you are and why.'*
>
> Mike Attridge, Needlemans

Figure 2.1 shows the type of records and information the *Supervisor* could collect for the *Project Manager* over and above that required by the *Supervisor*'s contractual role.

Figure 2.1 How the *Supervisor* could contribute to the project records and information

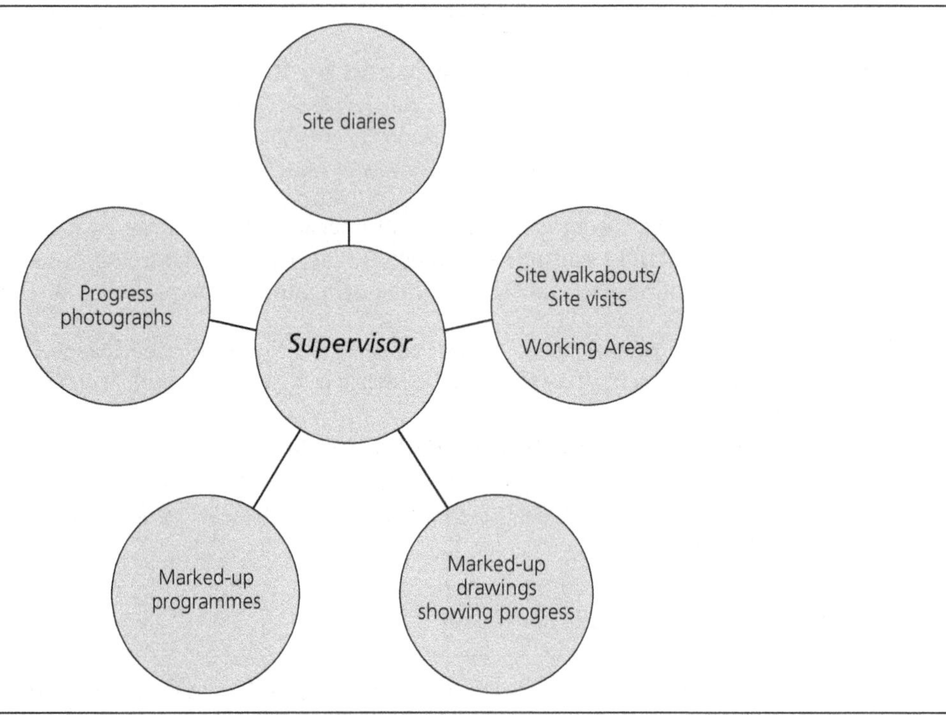

Figure 2.2 is an example of how the *Supervisor*'s records and information can be translated for the benefit of running a project.

2.3.2 Overview of the *Supervisor*'s personal contract with the *Employer*

This book refers frequently to the *Supervisor*'s personal contract with the *Employer*. The contract could be an ordinary staff employment contract which does not mention any of the *Supervisor*'s actions or it could be a contract for an outsourced *Supervisor*.

Figure 2.2 *Supervisor*'s interface with the *Project Manager*

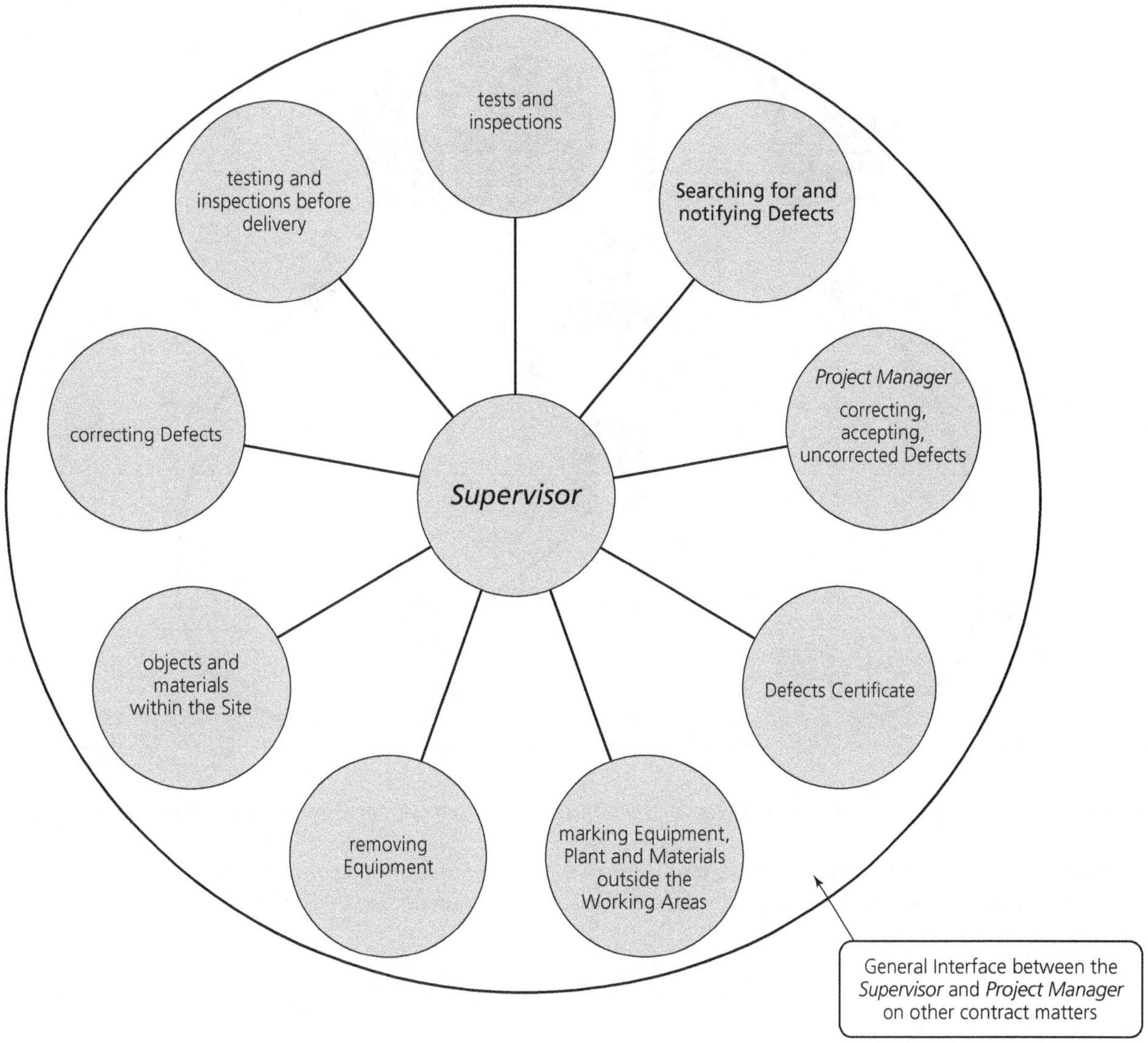

Staff employment contract

Where the *Supervisor* is a member of the *Employer*'s staff, it is unlikely that he will have been given special guidelines to adhere to in his role as *Supervisor*. However, he can access and deal with the *Employer*'s requirements easily through a normal line management structure. The *Supervisor* may wish to meet with the project sponsor, client and *Project Manager* to help him understand his remit and the extent of his role in the project.

Outsourced contract

Where the *Supervisor* has been outsourced and is a member of a consultancy firm (for example an engineering or project management company), he may need to be more rigorous and persistent in seeking guidance with regards to his role. The *Employer* has an opportunity to describe his requirements very precisely in the contract between the *Employer* and the consultancy firm – the *Supervisor*'s personal contract.

2.4.   The benefits brought by the *Supervisor*

An important part of the role which is often forgotten is that the *Supervisor* can act as the eyes and ears of the *Employer* and the *Project Manager* (see Figure 2.3).

This is not part of the role as defined in the ECC, but this requirement could be included as part of the scope of services in the *Supervisor*'s professional services contract. The *Supervisor* is in the perfect position to identify potential problems and prevent them happening or to use the contract to minimise that risk.

Figure 2.3 Eyes and ears on Site

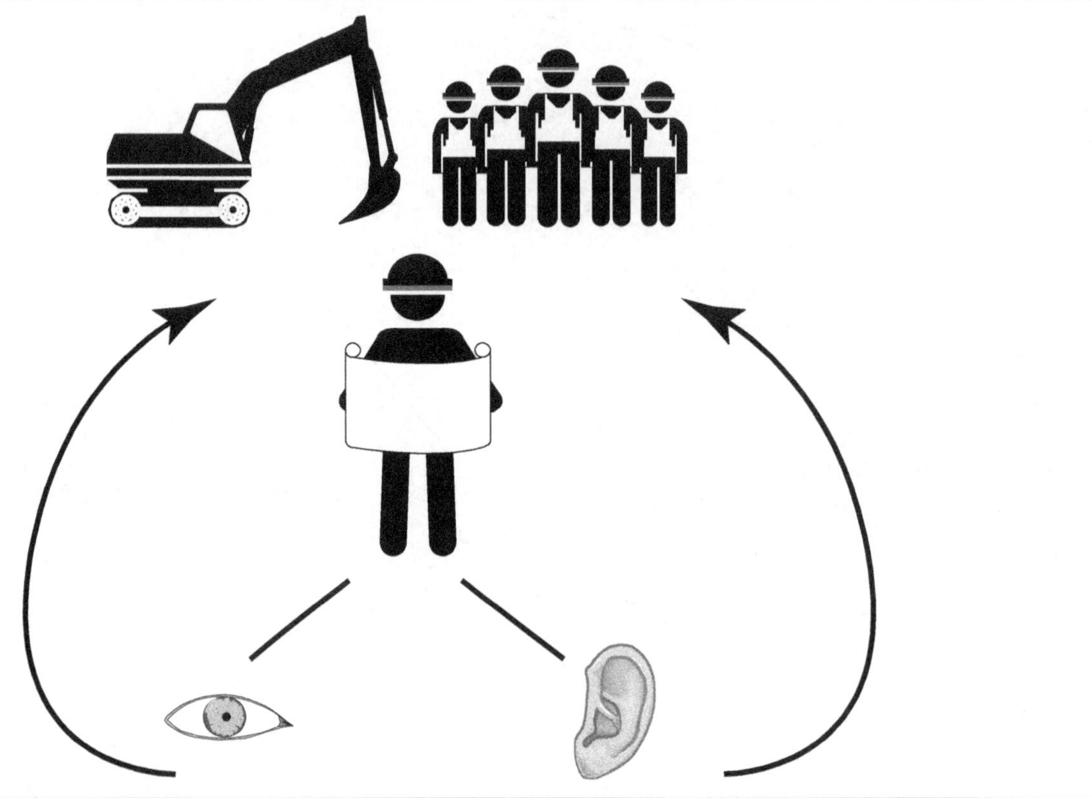

An important part of the effective management of the contract is a high standard of document and record-keeping.

Section 3 considers activities that need to be started prior to the *starting date* of the contract. It covers such topics as key procedures, communication protocols, checklists, Defects, tests and inspections, and marking.

Section 3

NEC3: The Role of the *Supervisor*
ISBN 978-0-7277-6096-8

Prior to the *starting date*

This section of the book focuses on the early stages of a project. In particular, it describes how the *Supervisor* can contribute to the pre-start activities to the benefit of the project.

3.1. The involvement of the *Supervisor*: introduction

An *Employer* will often contract with a quantity surveyor and a lead designer (e.g. architect) early on in the decision process for a project so that these professionals can contribute to the feasibility stage and add value to the business case. If the *Project Manager* and *Supervisor* roles are to be outsourced, as is so often the case, then the individuals taking on these roles are often not brought into the project until after the contract has been awarded.

It is true that the project procurement can be effective and efficient without a *Supervisor,* and that introducing the *Supervisor* at the last minute will not necessarily be detrimental to the project and its outcome. It is also recognised that every member of the project team can contribute to the project through their particular experience and specialism.

On a large project, where the role of *Supervisor* may be carried out by more than one individual (e.g. a civils *Supervisor* and an engineering services *Supervisor*), it can be beneficial to include the lead *Supervisor* as part of the project team from the start.

As the *Supervisor* concentrates primarily on the *works* and how it compares with the Works Information, it is helpful for the *Supervisor* to have early knowledge of the Works Information and the *Employer*'s objectives as expressed in the relevant documents. A *Supervisor* who is involved in the development of the Works Information will look at all the issues raised in section 3.2 and how best to express them in the Works Information.

3.2. On first reading of the Works Information: *Supervisor*'s checklist

This section primarily refers to the Works Information provided by the *Employer*, but the *Supervisor* will also need to read and understand any Works Information provided by the *Contractor*.

On first reading of the Works Information, it is recommended that the *Supervisor* identifies or isolates certain sections to go back to and review more thoroughly at a later date, after he has a feel for the Works Information as a whole and how it is composed.

It is likely that the *Supervisor* will find activities related to his role in most of the sections of the Works Information. For example (using the 'Example Works Information Structure' in *How to Write the ECC Works Information*), it may be inferred from heading WI 700 – Tests and inspections – that there is one place in which all tests and/or inspections will be listed; in practice, however, it is unlikely that all the information about tests and inspections will be found in one place in the Works Information, especially where the *Employer* makes reference to standards and guides in which tests are described.

3.2.1 Checklist: Tests and inspections

The ECC refers to tests and inspections required by the Works Information and the applicable law. The *Supervisor* could therefore review the Works Information and all the legislation and guidance it refers to in order to pull together a schedule of tests/inspections and in what part of the programme they will be required.

The checklists in this section were compiled using the checklist provided in *How to Write the ECC Works Information.*

<table>
<tr><td>Checklist 1: Tests/inspections schedule</td><td>✓</td></tr>
</table>

- Name of test/inspection
- Reason for taking the test/inspection
- Any procedures or notes if it is a repeat test/inspection
- When it is to take place (date or timing of the *works*)
- Whether the work is going to be covered up
- How much notice is to be provided by the *Contractor*
- Where it is to take place
- Who is to carry out the test/inspection
- Who else is to be in attendance
- Involvement of specialists
- Whether the *Contractor* watches or takes part
- Documents to be used or provided for the test/inspection and who is required to provide them
- Any procedures to be adhered to
- What the access requirements are and what procedures are in place to gain access
- What the test environment is required to be and any procedures for putting it in place
- What method is to be used in carrying out the test/inspection
- Any information or instructions required to be provided for the test/inspection, by whom and for whom
- Any Equipment required and who is to provide it and what timescales are required to get it
- Any materials, facilities and samples to be provided to carry out the test and who is to provide them and how much notice do they need
- What standards are to be used in determining the results
- What results are acceptable and any deviations/tolerances which may be acceptable
- What communications are required to the *Employer* or *Project Manager* with regards to failed tests/inspections
- What documents are to be produced after the test, who produces them and to whom are they sent/copied
- Whether or not authorisation to proceed to the next stage of the work depends on the test results
- What information/documentation the *Project Manager* and the *Employer* want to see regarding the test/inspection

<table>
<tr><td>Checklist 2: Information about tests/inspections in the Works Information</td><td>✓</td></tr>
</table>

- Look for the requirement to produce a schedule and whether the *Project Manager* expects to see it and manage it as part of his duties. The *Supervisor* may be required to submit the schedule to the *Project Manager* and follow any instructions the *Project Manager* may require with regards to changes or regular submissions.
- Samples of Plant or Materials provided by the *Contractor* which the *Supervisor* may be required to check or test – what are they, when are they to be provided, when are they required to be used as a comparison, where are they stored?
- Samples of workmanship to be used as a comparison basis – in what part of the *works* (or Works for a different contract), when will they take place, how are they to be used?
- Equipment, Plant and Materials outside the Working Areas which the *Supervisor* is required to test/inspect before payment or delivery – timetable, description, access?
- What facilities, samples and materials the *Employer* is intending to provide for tests/inspections – what are they, where are they to be found, how much notice does the *Employer* need, what communications is the *Employer* expecting from the *Supervisor*?
- Method statements or risk assessments required from the *Contractor* which may result in optional or follow-on tests/inspections.

<table>
<tr><td>

Checklist 2: Continued

</td><td>✓</td></tr>
<tr><td>

- Tests/inspections which are perhaps routine and not specifically mentioned in the Works Information (but should be included), such as checks of materials (e.g. aggregate) or testing mortar.
- Tests/inspections which may clash in terms of when they will take place or things required – discussions with the *Project Manager* in the first place, and the *Contractor* to resolve.
- Any other parties involved in the test/inspection process, such as representatives from special bodies (e.g. Environment Agency), and the communications required from the *Supervisor* with regards to notice or test results.
- Tests/inspections to be undertaken after take over but before the *defects date* – part of checklist 1, but check for any prior setup requirements.
- Tests/inspections which the *Supervisor* may need others to do if they are outside of his expertise (e.g. software).
- Tests/inspections to be undertaken by the *Contractor* or external bodies which the *Supervisor* wants to watch or be a part of.
- Tests/inspections which may take place over a period of time (e.g. performance tests) – part of checklist 1, but check for any prior setup requirements.
- Performance tests required for secondary Option X17, Low performance damages – part of checklist 1, but check for what needs to happen beforehand so that the procedures are smooth going into the performance test.
- Any tests/inspections on the *Contractor*'s design which may be required.

</td><td></td></tr>
</table>

3.2.2 Checklist: Marking

The ECC clause 71.1 requires the *Contractor* to prepare items for marking and the contract to identify those same items for payment. The *Supervisor* will not be required to undertake marking for all contracts. However, unless his personal contract is very clear, the *Supervisor* should look for indications in the Works Information that the *Contractor* is required to prepare Equipment, Plant and Materials for marking.

<table>
<tr><td>

Checklist 3: Marking

</td><td>✓</td></tr>
<tr><td>

- If not specifically said, does it seem as if the *Supervisor* is required to mark Equipment, Plant and Materials?
- Are vesting certificates required?
- Check the Works Information for references to payment for Equipment, Plant and Materials and, where there is no mention, check the *activity schedule* or the *bill of quantities* (or perhaps even the Schedule of Cost Components) for references to payment for Equipment, Plant and Materials.
- How is the *Contractor* to prepare Equipment, Plant and Materials for marking?
- How is marking of Equipment, Plant and Materials for payment to take place?
- How is marking of Plant and Materials to take place for title purposes?
- Where is it to take place?
- What preparations are necessary for the marking?
- Are any tests/inspections to be done prior to marking?
- What procedures are required for marking?
- What records/photos are required?

</td><td></td></tr>
</table>

3.2.3 Checklist: Defects

The definition of Defects is in relation to the Works Information, therefore the *Supervisor* should have read and be aware of the whole of the Works Information, even if not all of it is applicable to the *Supervisor*'s direct activities.

<table>
<tr><td>

Checklist 4: Defects

</td><td>✓</td></tr>
<tr><td>

- Note those areas of work to review and monitor closely on Site.
- Ask to see any method statements or any risk assessments by the *Contractor* as these will help identify potential Defects.

</td><td>✓</td></tr>
</table>

<table>
<tr><td>Checklist 4: Continued</td><td>✓</td></tr>
</table>

- Note what aspects of the *works* will be carried out by Subcontractors and the actual checks by the *Contractor* against his accepted quality management system.
- Note any checks required against the *Contractor*'s design.
- Check for a description of the work which has to be done to reach Completion.
- Note any definition of Completion in the Works Information for comparison against the *works* especially when approaching Completion.
- Check for Defects that would prevent the *Employer* using the *works* and Others from doing their work.
- Check for any tests that are to be done at or around Completion or to reach Completion.
- Check for access arrangements for any Defects after take over.

3.2.4 Checklist: Quality management system required from the *Contractor*

There is no direct reference in the ECC to the *Contractor* having or developing a quality management system; however, the Works Information may state some requirements regarding quality (see also section 3.2.6 regarding the Works Information for the *Contractor*'s design).

<table>
<tr><td>Checklist 5: Requirements for a quality management system</td><td>✓</td></tr>
</table>

- Any references in the Works Information to the *Contractor*'s own QMS or to legislation, guidance (e.g. BS EN ISO 9001: 2008) or accreditations.
- Any references in the Works Information provided for the *Contractor*'s design to describe how his QMS meets the requirements of the Works Information provided by the *Employer*.
- Review of the *Contractor*'s quality procedures that will take place in the Working Areas and outside the Working Areas for Equipment, Plant and Materials, especially those which the *Supervisor* may be required to test/inspect prior to marking and delivery, such as how he plans to implement the work (method statement) and quality plan, quality audits and management of non-conformances.
- Samples of Plant and Materials against which the quality of the *works* will be measured and monitored.
- Any procedures for engaging with the *Contractor* for submission of samples and acceptance and/or interaction with the *Project Manager* and *Employer*.
- Any areas of the *works* where the *Contractor*'s QMS may be required, particularly where it corresponds with the *Supervisor*'s procedures for Defects, for example, checking Subcontractors' work and areas of the *works* prior to tests required by the *Supervisor* or by legislation.
- References to samples that the *Contractor* is required to provide to be used as a comparison basis. If the *Supervisor* is not mentioned with regards to the receipt and examination of the samples, then find out about procedures from the *Project Manager* so that it is clear what to look for.

3.2.5 Checklist: Personal duties for the *Supervisor*

There may be other duties that the *Supervisor* is required to carry out and which are described in the Works Information. If the *Employer* has not synchronised the Works Information and the personal contract with the *Supervisor*, then the *Supervisor* may need to take notes of activities required by the Works Information and approach the *Employer* to clarify any discrepancies.

<table>
<tr><td>Checklist 6: Personal duties as Supervisor</td><td>✓</td></tr>
</table>

- Note any areas in the Works Information that require actions of the *Supervisor* that are not generally required of a *Supervisor*.
- Check any anomalies with the *Supervisor*'s professional services contract.
- Tag any areas in the Works Information that involve duties that would be additional to the *Supervisor*'s professional services contract.
- Approach the *Employer* and/or the *Project Manager* to seek clarification of anomalies.

3.2.6 Checklist: Works Information provided by the *Contractor* for his design

Works Information provided by the *Contractor* for his design will not be present in every contract. Whether it is included in the contract depends on the *Employer*'s procurement processes, the type of contract and contract strategy, and the main Option chosen.

Checklist 7: Works Information provided for the *Contractor*'s design	✓
■ The *Employer* should ensure that there are no ambiguities or inconsistencies between his Works Information and the part of the *Contractor*'s submitted tender which is being incorporated into the contract as Works Information provided by the *Contractor* for his design. However, the *Supervisor* may choose to review both documents from his own point of view so that he understands how the *Contractor* is proposing to construct the *works* and how he is going to approach the parts of the contract that affect the *Supervisor*.	
■ Mark or tag any actual or potential anomalies for discussion with the *Employer*, the *Project Manager* or the *Contractor*.	
■ Mark any areas of design that will be compared against the *works*.	
■ Briefly check all guidelines and regulations to ensure familiarity and clarify any standards required.	

3.3. The *Supervisor*'s procedures

The breadth and depth of the *Supervisor*'s activities will be determined by his contract with the *Employer*. As the *Supervisor* reports to the *Employer* (rather than the *Project Manager*), the *Employer* is sure to want updates and information from the *Supervisor* at regular intervals. This requirement should be included in the *Supervisor*'s contract, along with any obligations that are not required by the ECC. In particular, if the *Employer* wants the *Supervisor* to keep a site diary, notes on progress and detailed records (including photos), then the *Employer* needs to describe this requirement in the *Supervisor*'s contract as the ECC does not require these documents from the *Supervisor*. Similarly, any regular contact with the *Project Manager* should also be described in the *Supervisor*'s professional services contract.

3.3.1 Site diaries and other project records

A detailed discussion about site diaries is presented in section 4.13.2 of this book.

The recording of progress on Site and other information and events, if required by the *Supervisor*'s personal contract, will need a disciplined approach. For this to be done well, time must be set aside every day to review the day's work and record information about the Working Areas (the Site and other areas used to Provide the Works), the weather, deliveries, resources used and so on.

It is recommended that the *Supervisor* sets up his own procedures for recording information, and that on a larger project he enforces these procedures by using delegates and other members of the supervisory team. Even if the *Employer* does not require records, and the keeping of records is not part of the *Supervisor*'s personal contract, the *Supervisor* may choose to keep a diary to help him keep track of daily activities.

The *Supervisor* will also keep records of Defects, tests and inspections and marking (see sections 3.2.1 to 3.2.3).

3.3.2 Communications: general

Communication is the key to any well-managed project. Clause 13 of the ECC clearly sets out the rules for communications that the *Supervisor* must follow. It states:

■ that communications must be in a form which can be 'read, copied and recorded' (e.g. in writing)
■ that any notifications must be separate communications
■ the language to be used
■ the address to be used (but the parties can agree a less formal address, e.g. email)
■ the period within which a reply must be made
■ who should receive certificates
■ that acceptance of a communication by the *Supervisor* does not dilute the *Contractor*'s responsibilities.

3.3.3 Communications: ECC communications from the *Supervisor*

The ECC requires the following communications from the *Supervisor*, as shown in Table 3.1.

Table 3.1 ECC communications from the *Supervisor*

Notification	Receiver	Copied to	Other rules
Defects Certificate – clauses 11.2(6) and 43.3	*Contractor*	*Project Manager*	■ Clause 13.1 – writing ■ Clause 13.1 – language ■ Clause 13.2 – address notified ■ Clause 13.7 – communicated separately
Notice of delegation – clause 14.2	*Contractor*	Not required	
Notice cancelling delegation – clause 14.2	*Contractor*	Not required	
Instruction – clause 27.3	*Contractor*	Not required (but good practice to copy to the *Project Manager*)	
Test/inspection notification – clause 40.3	*Contractor*	Not required (but good practice to advise the *Project Manager* for a significant test)	
Test/inspection results – clause 40.3	*Contractor*	Not required (but good practice to advise the *Project Manager* for a significant test)	
Plant and Materials passed tests – clause 41.1	*Contractor*	Not required	
Instruction to search for a Defect – clause 42.1	*Contractor*	Not required	
Defect notification – clause 42.2	*Contractor*	Not required	

3.3.4 Communications: ECC communications to the *Supervisor*

The ECC requires the following communications to be issued to the *Supervisor*, as shown in Table 3.2.

Table 3.2 ECC communications to the *Supervisor*

Notification	Sender	Response required?	Other rules
Instruction to attend a risk reduction meeting – clause 16.2	*Contractor* or *Project Manager*	Not required	No rules for the *Supervisor*; sender should adhere to usual rules of communication
Test/inspection notification – clause 40.3	*Contractor*	Not required	■ Clause 13.1 – writing ■ Clause 13.1 – language ■ Clause 13.2 – address notified ■ Clause 13.7 – communicated separately
Test/inspection results – clause 40.3	*Contractor*	Not required	
Defect notification – clause 42.2	*Contractor*	Not required	

3.3.5   Communications: non-ECC communications involving the *Supervisor*

Communications that are not required by the ECC but which the people operating the contract might consider include those shown in Table 3.3.

Table 3.3 Non-ECC communications involving the *Supervisor*

Communication	Reason for communication
Early warning notice	The *Supervisor* sees something that may increase the Prices, affect the programme or impair the performance of the *works*.
Changing the Working Areas	The *Supervisor* thinks that the *Contractor* is not sticking to the Working Areas, or that the *Contractor* could make good use of another location.
Notification of ambiguity or inconsistency	The *Supervisor* thinks there is an ambiguity or inconsistency in or between the contract documents.
Notice of illegal or impossible Works Information	The *Supervisor* thinks that the Works Information requires the *Contractor* to do something that is illegal or impossible.
Removal of *Contractor*'s people from Site	The *Supervisor* thinks that an employee of the *Contractor* is not contributing to the project or is causing difficulties and the project would benefit from his removal from the Site.
Notification to provide items for tests/inspections	The *Supervisor* wants to advise the *Employer* that he has scheduled a test/inspection and the *Employer* will need to provide the materials, facilities and samples stated in the Works Information.
Notification of test/inspection costs	It is the *Project Manager*'s duty to compile costs for repeating a test/inspection; however, the *Supervisor* may be able to provide accurate information quickly and the *Project Manager* may choose to request the *Supervisor*'s help in carrying out this duty.
Notification that access is required after take over – clause 43.4	It is the *Project Manager* who is required to notify the *Employer* that the *Contractor* needs access to correct a Defect. However, given that the *Supervisor* is the one who receives or issues a Defect notification, it is more likely to be the *Supervisor* who advises the *Project Manager* and possibly the *Employer*.
Notification to the *Supervisor* about Equipment, Plant and Materials outside the Working Areas	The *Contractor* is not required to notify the *Supervisor* that he has prepared items for marking (clause 71.1) but it would be helpful if notification took place.
Notification of marking (vesting certificate)	The *Supervisor* may choose to advise the *Employer* and the *Project Manager* (as well as the *Contractor*) that he has marked the required Plant and Materials which are outside the Working Areas and therefore title has passed to the *Employer* (clause 70.1).
Marking Equipment, Plant and Materials	The *Supervisor* may choose to notify the *Contractor* and the *Project Manager* that he has marked Equipment, Plant and Materials outside the Working Area (clause 71.1) and therefore the *Contractor* may now expect payment to be included in the next payment certificate.

Table 3.3 Continued

Communication	Reason for communication
Notification of Plant and Materials delivery	The *Contractor* may choose to notify the *Supervisor* and/or the *Project Manager* that Plant and Materials have been moved to the Working Areas and he can do the same for Equipment (clause 70.2).
Notification of free issue Plant and Materials	The *Project Manager* or the *Supervisor* may be given the duty to notify the *Contractor* that free issue Plant and Materials have been delivered to the Site; or one of them may advise the *Contractor* of the details to arrange delivery of the items himself.

Section 4

NEC3: The Role of the *Supervisor*
ISBN 978-0-7277-6096-8

ICE Publishing: All rights reserved
http://dx.doi.org/10.1680/nectrs.60968.047

From the *starting date* to Completion

This section details the tasks that the *Supervisor* is required to carry out from the start of the construction phase of a project until the date on which the *Project Manager* certifies that Completion has taken place. In addition to the procedures regarding tests/inspections, Defects and marking, there are other activities that the *Supervisor* can undertake and which add value to the contract as a whole.

4.1. Understanding the terms: Defects

Defects	■ Defect is a defined term. It has two strands:
	  – work which is not in accordance with the Works Information or the applicable law
	  – a part of the *works* designed by the *Contractor* which is not in accordance with the applicable law or the *Contractor*'s design which the *Project Manager* has accepted.
	■ Defects can be notified up to the *defects date*.
	■ There is no contractual restriction on the date before which Defects may not be notified.
	■ The *Supervisor*'s procedures when dealing with Defects notified before Completion are detailed in section 4.10 of this book.

defect correction period	■ For Defects notified before Completion, the *defect correction period* starts at Completion.
	■ For Defects notified after Completion, the *defect correction period* starts when the Defect is notified.
	■ Notified Defects must be corrected within their *defect correction period*.
	■ The use of italics in the term *defect correction period* indicates that the parties can find the timescale in the Contract Data.
	■ Contract Data part one provides the *defect correction period*, which may appear as one period for all Defects (e.g. two weeks), or as a series of periods based on the categorisation of Defects. The *Contractor*'s obligations on discovery of a Defect are set out in clause 43:
	  – The *Contractor* is required to correct within the *defect correction period* all Defects which are notified by the *Supervisor*.
	  – The *Contractor* is required to correct within the *defect correction period* all Defects which are notified by the *Contractor*.
	  – The Contractor is required to correct all Defects even if they have not been notified, but the period for correction is not provided in the ECC (more on this later in this section).

tests/inspections	■ The procedures regarding tests/inspections are relevant only to tests/inspections required by the Works Information or the applicable law.
marking	■ The process and method of marking is not prescribed in the ECC and therefore should be described in the Works Information and/or the *Supervisor*'s contract.
Working Areas	■ The Working Areas are described by the *Contractor* in his Contract Data part two and they can be added to (clause 15.1). ■ The Working Areas must be necessary to Provide the Works and they must be used only for work in the contract, which means that the *Contractor*'s common areas of working cannot be included in the Woking Areas. ■ The Working Areas include the Site.

4.2. Collaborative working

As with other roles, the *Supervisor* can impact positively on the contract or not. A *Supervisor* who engages with the *Contractor* and others around him will help the output of the contract by working together and easing the workload for all. One who does not work collaboratively and simply bats problems back to the *Contractor* with no input will not add positively to the contract, and can therefore make the output harder for everybody.

Figure 4.1 Collaborative working within the ECC

Actions for the *Supervisor*	To-do list for the *Supervisor*
■ Act in a spirit of mutual trust and co-operation. ■ Work with the *Project Manager*, the *Contractor* and the *Employer* in the spirit of the contract, beyond the words in and actions required by the contract. ■ Communicate with all those involved in the contract so that there are no surprises. ■ Adhere to the *Supervisor*'s personal contract, as well as performing the *Supervisor*'s actions under the ECC.	■ Be familiar with the rights and obligations of all those with whom the *Supervisor* is required to interact under the contract.

4.3. Works Information

All of the *Supervisor*'s primary duties of Defect notification, undertaking and watching tests/inspections and marking refer to the Works Information (directly or indirectly).

- Clause 40 applies to tests and inspections required by the Works Information (clause 40.1) and therefore all other references in clause 40 also refer to the tests/inspections described in the Works Information, for example:
  - notification (clause 40.3)
  - Defect manifested (clause 40.4).
- The *Employer* is required to provide materials, facilities and samples for tests and inspections as stated in the Works Information (clause 40.2).
- The Plant and Materials to be tested are as stated in the Works Information (clause 41.1).
- Searching can include tests and inspections which the Works Information does not require (clause 42.1).
- Definition of a Defect refers to the Works Information (clause 11.2(5) and clause 42.1).
- The Works Information describes how and when the *Supervisor* should mark Plant and Materials outside the Working Areas (clause 70.1).
- The Works Information describes how the *Contractor* should prepare any Equipment, Plant and Materials for marking which is to be carried out by the *Supervisor* (clause 71.1).

The *Supervisor* therefore needs to be very familiar with the Works Information. In some cases, the *Supervisor*'s knowledge (and that of his team) must be more detailed than the *Project Manager*'s, which can allow the *Project Manager* to concentrate on the programme and budget.

The *Supervisor* must be cognisant of both the Works Information provided by the *Employer* and the Works Information the *Contractor* provided with his tender and which forms part of the contract. The Works Information provided by the

Contractor may include tests/inspections and other details of how the *Contractor* plans to carry out the *works* and what procedures he may follow in doing so.

The *Supervisor* must understand that the Works Information is the primary reference document for most of his actions. For example, a Defect is (inter alia) a part of the *works* which is not in accordance with the Works Information (clause 11.5(5)); therefore, the *Supervisor* may only compare the *works* with the requirements of the Works Information, rather than with his preferred construction. Where the Works Information is output-based, the *Supervisor* must accept the way the *works* have been constructed if the specified output is met, even if the *Supervisor* does not like the way it has been done. Section 3 of this book details more about the Works Information.

<table>
<tr><td>

Actions for the *Supervisor*

- Prior to notifying a Defect, make sure that any part of the *works* which the *Supervisor* considers to be incorrect or defective is actually a Defect as defined.
- Let the *Project Manager* know if the *Supervisor* thinks that there is a part of the *works* which is incorrect or will not contribute to the objectives of the contract, even if this part of the *works* is not a Defect as defined.
- Let the *Project Manager* know if the *Supervisor* intends to instruct a search or instruct a way of carrying out the *works* which is not required by the Works Information (that is actions which may result in a compensation event).

</td><td>

To-do list for the *Supervisor*

- Become familiar with the Works Information.
- Separately list or mark on the programme when tests/inspections are required to take place.
- Particularly note tests/inspections which need to be passed before a payment is made to the *Contractor*.
- Note when the *Employer* is required to provide materials, facilities and samples for tests/inspections so that the *Supervisor* can facilitate that these things are ready in time to carry out the test/inspection.

</td></tr>
</table>

4.4. Programme requirements

The practicalities of drafting and maintaining the programme are sufficiently dealt with by the core clauses of the ECC and there are no direct duties for the *Supervisor* in this part of the contract. But the *Supervisor* is affected by the Accepted Programme and the *Supervisor* can influence the programme and the progress of the *works*.

<table>
<tr><td>

Impact of the Accepted Programme

</td><td>

Supervisor* actions which affect the programme of the *works

</td></tr>
<tr><td>

The *Supervisor* should make sure that his schedule is based around the Accepted Programme and that his activities take account of:
- dates
- the order and timing of the *works* – how the *Contractor* plans to undertake the *works* – so that the *Supervisor* can plan where he needs to be on the Site at certain times
- procedures – any programmed provisions for Defects or tests/inspections
- dates when the *Contractor* will need things from the *Employer* to carry out tests/inspections or Plant and Materials outside the Working Areas
- method and resource statements – so that the *Supervisor* can compare them with what is actually taking place (see section 3.3.1 on recording information)
- requirements included in the Works Information (bearing in mind that this may be substantial, depending on the type of *works*, its complexity and the risks involved) which may affect the *Supervisor*'s required actions.

</td><td>

The *Supervisor*'s actions can affect the progress of the *works* if:
- the *Contractor* prepares Plant and Materials for marking as the Works Information requires but the *Supervisor* does not mark them timeously
- a search instructed by the *Supervisor* does not reveal a Defect (caveats in clause 60.1(10))
- the *Supervisor* delays carrying out a test/inspection
- the *Supervisor* does not notify a Defect timeously (note that this does not remove the *Contractor*'s duty to correct all Defects)
- the *Supervisor* incorrectly notifies a Defect or notifies a failed test because his requirements are more stringent than those envisaged by the Works Information
- they are any of the compensation events listed in clause 60.1.

</td></tr>
</table>

4.5. Key risks

The management of project risks is the responsibility of all parties involved in the contract, including the *Supervisor*. The ECC does not detail obligations for the *Supervisor* with regard to risks, but the *Supervisor*'s contract may require actions and interactions for the *Supervisor* which contribute towards the *Project Manager*'s management of project risks and those risks included on the Risk Register.

The Risk Register is managed by the *Project Manager* and contains (1) risks which were listed in the Contract Data, and (2) risks which have been notified as early warning matters by the *Contractor* or the *Project Manager*. Clause 11.2(14) also states what must be included on the Risk Register for each risk: description of the risk and mitigating actions.

There are likely to be some risks which affect the *Supervisor* – for example, things that he needs to look out for on the Site – and ways in which he increases the risk to the programme. There are also likely to be matters which the *Supervisor* considers to be risks but which are not included in the Risk Register. Many of the *Supervisor*'s actions, such as notifying Defects and carrying out tests/inspections, can affect the programme, the budget and the quality of the *works*.

<table>
<tr><td>

Actions for the *Supervisor*

- Advise the *Project Manager* where the *Supervisor* thinks that a new risk has arisen or where a risk has been avoided.
- Advise the *Project Manager* where Defects and/or tests/inspections have revealed a matter critical to the programme or budget or quality of the *works*.
- Ask the *Project Manager* if there are any actions which the *Supervisor* can undertake which will mitigate risks in the Risk Register or will help manage them.

</td><td>

To-do list for the *Supervisor*

- Be familiar with the Risk Register and make a note of those risks which either affect the *Supervisor* or which he can affect.
- Check his personal contract for any specific actions required with regard to early warnings.

</td></tr>
</table>

4.6. Early warnings

The early warning procedure is detailed in clause 16. As with the Risk Register (which is part of the early warning procedure and therefore is also detailed in clause 16), there are no detailed obligations of the *Supervisor*. However, the management of risks and therefore early warnings is the responsibility of all those who take part in the contract, including the *Supervisor*. The *Supervisor*'s personal contract may also require actions and interactions for the *Supervisor* that contribute towards the *Project Manager*'s management of project risks and early warnings.

<table>
<tr><td>

Actions for the *Supervisor*

- Advise the *Project Manager* where the *Supervisor* thinks that something will affect the budget, programme or quality of the *works*.
- Attend any risk reduction meetings which the *Contractor* or the *Project Manager* has instructed him to attend and take part in the discussions.
- Take part in any meetings and discussions which the *Supervisor*'s personal contract requires him to, including regular meetings between the *Project Manager* and the *Supervisor* to keep the *Project Manager* informed of how the *works* are progressing.

</td><td>

To-do list for the *Supervisor*

- Understand the early warning procedure and the roles of the *Contractor* and the *Project Manager* in that procedure.
- Check the *Supervisor*'s personal contract for any specific actions required with regard to early warnings.

</td></tr>
</table>

4.7. Compensation events

The compensation event procedure detailed in section 6 of the core clauses is the most important contract procedure in the ECC in that it details how change is managed. Once again, the *Supervisor* has no direct input to the procedure, although his actions can be the cause of change and can be notified as a compensation event. It is therefore recommended that the *Supervisor*'s personal contract details how the *Supervisor* should interact with the *Project Manager* with regard to compensation events and what actions are required to facilitate the effective end to the procedure, especially where the *Supervisor*'s actions have caused a compensation event.

4.7.1 Compensation events related to the *Supervisor*

Table 4.1 Compensation events related to the *Supervisor*

Clause	Description	Comments
60.1(6)	The *Supervisor* does not reply to a communication from the *Contractor* within the period required by the contract. This clause interacts with clause 13.3: If the contract requires the *Supervisor* to reply to a communication, he replies within the *period for reply*.	■ The *period for reply* is stated in Contract Data part one, e.g. two weeks. ■ While this may be regarded as the default *period for reply*, there may be other communications within the Works Information for which the stated time period is different. ■ The ECC does not include for any *Contractor* communications to which the *Supervisor* must reply, therefore for this compensation event to be activated, there must be communication requirements in the Works Information or the Option Z clauses.
60.1(8)	The *Supervisor* changes a decision which he had previously communicated.	■ There is no explicit clause under the ECC according to which the *Supervisor* makes and communicates a decision. ■ Some readers may choose to infer that some actions require decisions and that, for example, the *Supervisor* can change his decision that a part of the *works* contains a Defect (clause 42.2).

Example of a changed decision:
The *Supervisor* hereby notifies the *Contractor* of a changed decision in relation to Notified Defect No 423/4 that this is NOT a Defect. The reason for the changed decision is because the *Contractor* has provided further evidence that a Defect does not exist.

Clause	Description	Comments
60.1(10)	The *Supervisor* instructs the *Contractor* to search for a Defect and no Defect is found unless the search is needed only because the *Contractor* gave insufficient notice of doing work obstructing a required test or inspection. This clause interacts with: ■ clause 42.1: The *Supervisor* may instruct the *Contractor* to search for a Defect ■ clause 40.3: The *Contractor* notifies the *Supervisor* in time for a test or inspection to be arranged and done before doing work which would obstruct the test or inspection.	■ Although clause 60.1(10) gives the *Contractor* the right to notify a clause 42.1 search as a compensation event, there are strict parameters in place to discourage abuse by both the *Supervisor* and the *Contractor*, as well as the omnipotent requirement for 'mutual trust and co-operation'. ■ The flow chart in Figure 4.2 describes the interaction of the clauses. ■ Note that if a Defect is found, the *Supervisor* may not force immediate correction. This is further mentioned in section 4.10.3.

Example of an instruction to search:
The *Contractor* is hereby instructed to open up the *works* to search for a Defect. The search is needed **only** because the *Contractor* did not give sufficient notice of doing work which now obstructs a required test or inspection.

Clause	Description	Comments
60.1(11)	A test or inspection by the *Supervisor* causes unnecessary delay. This clause interacts with clause 40.5: The *Supervisor* does his tests and inspections without causing unnecessary delay.	■ Since the *Supervisor* is required to undertake his tests/inspections without causing unnecessary delay, it makes sense that any tardiness can be notified as a compensation event. ■ 'Unnecessary delay' is not defined and there is further discussion about this phrase in section 4.11. ■ An example of delay could be where a test undertaken by the *Supervisor* takes longer than planned, but this might not be classed an 'unnecessary delay'.

Figure 4.2 Flow chart for instructing a search for a Defect

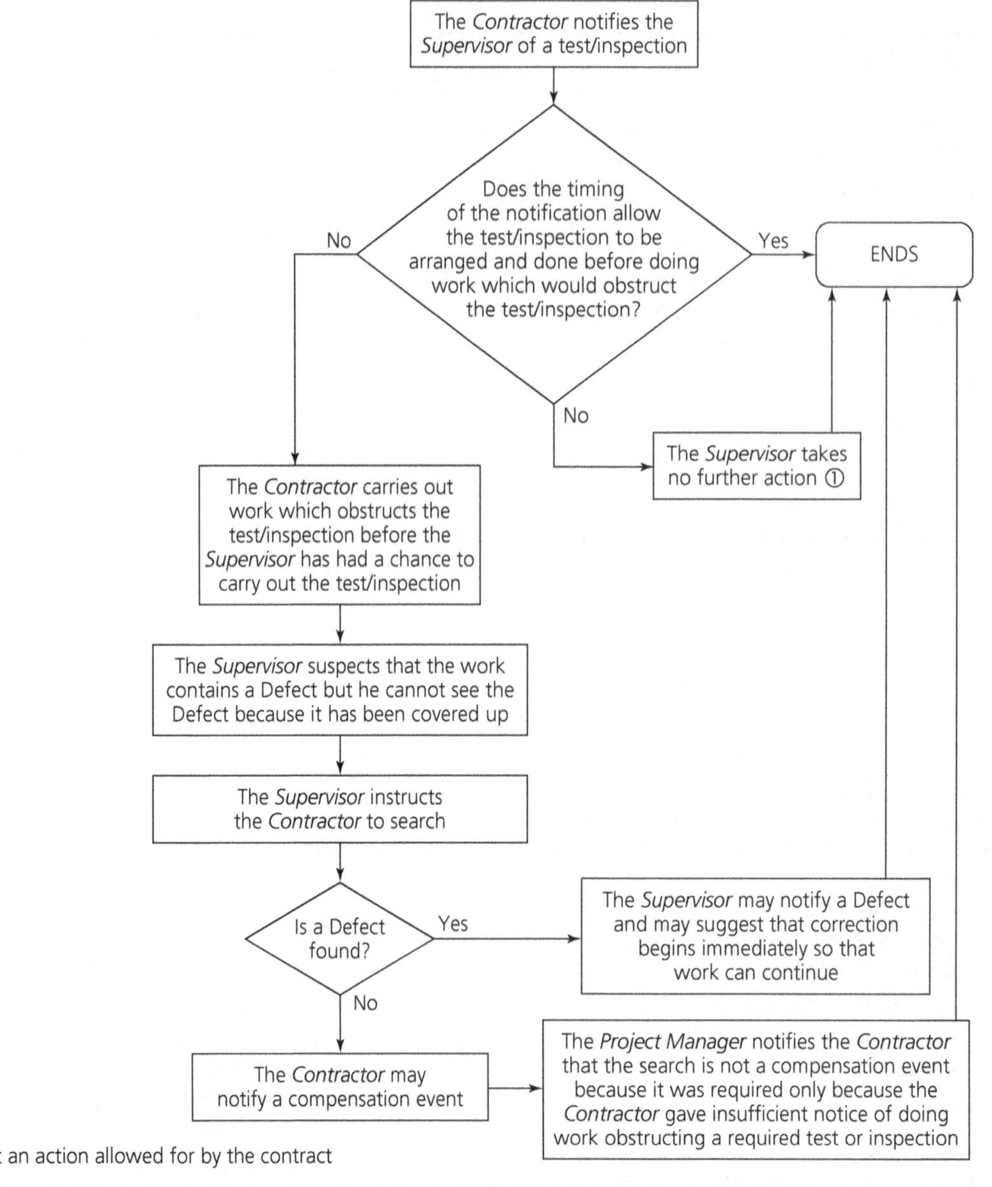

4.7.2   Clause 40.5

Clause 40.5 is not a compensation event, but it is included here as it includes a non-action by the *Supervisor* and its consequences to the *Employer*. The payment required is not as severe as the consequences of a compensation event could be.

The clause contains two requirements and this section discusses the second requirement only. The first requirement (to carry out tests/inspections without causing unnecessary delay) is discussed at section 4.11.

Clause 40.5   The *Supervisor* does his tests and inspections without causing unnecessary delay to work or to a payment which is conditional upon a test or inspection being successful. A payment which is conditional upon a *Supervisor*'s test or inspection being successful becomes due at the later of the *defects date* and the end of the last *defect correction period* if:

- the *Supervisor* has not done the test or inspection and
- the delay to the test or inspection is not the *Contractor*'s fault.

The clause refers to:

- a test/inspection required by either the Works Information or the applicable law and
- a payment which is conditional upon that test/inspection being successful and

- the *Supervisor* not doing the test/inspection and
- the delay to the test/inspection not being the *Contractor*'s fault then
- the payment becomes due to the *Contractor* anyway.

The clause refers to the *Supervisor* not having done the test/inspection and the 'delay' not being the *Contractor*'s fault. The difference between not doing the test at all and a delay in doing the test is not clear; and the clause seems to suggest that the *Supervisor* not having done the test by the time of the *defects date* is tardy rather than an omission. The ramifications are not affected by the interpretation, however; and not doing the test by the *defects date* means that the payment becomes due to the *Contractor* even if the test has not been done. Any other consequences of not doing the test, such as finding a Defect, may be included in the Risk Register and may be the responsibility of the *Project Manager*.

<table>
<tr><td>

Actions for the *Supervisor*

- Before giving an instruction, make sure that the *Project Manager* is aware of the matter and the instruction so that he can assess the situation and any resulting compensation event.
- Make sure that the *Project Manager* is advised of any searches so that he can manage the programme and budget of the project.

</td><td>

To-do list for the *Supervisor*

- Be familiar with all the *periods for reply* included in the contract, especially where there are categories of communication rather than just one *period for reply*.
- Be familiar with all the actions that impact on a search.

</td></tr>
</table>

4.7.3 How compensation events affect the *Supervisor*

The *Supervisor* should be aware that compensation events may affect the programme of the *works*, whether or not the Completion Date is changed. He should ensure that communication lines are open to the *Project Manager* so that he [the *Supervisor*] is aware of any changes to the Accepted Programme. For example, a compensation event may affect:

- the order or timing of events, such that the *Supervisor*'s testing/inspection schedule needs to change
- the number of tests/inspections
- the type of test/inspection and who carries it out
- the way the event or the test/inspection is carried out (method statement).

4.8. Dispute resolution

The *Supervisor* is not directly involved in the dispute resolution procedure, but his actions or lack of actions during the contract can lead to a dispute.

The *Supervisor* should be aware of the following.

- Any action or lack of action by the *Supervisor* may lead to a dispute.
- The *Adjudicator* may review or revise any action or inaction of the *Supervisor* as required.
- During any dispute, all parties working under the contract proceed as if there were no dispute.
- The failure by the *Supervisor* to act as stated in the contract will leave him open to possible action for breach of services by the *Employer* under his personal contract.

> **Key message**
>
> The failure by the *Supervisor* to act as stated in the contract will leave him open to possible action for breach of services by the *Employer*.

<table>
<tr><td>

Actions for the *Supervisor*

- Be aware that everything the *Supervisor* does and everything which he ought to do may lead to a dispute and may be scrutinised by the *Adjudicator*.
- Carry on with the contract even if a dispute has been notified.

</td><td>

To-do list for the *Supervisor*

- Be aware of the dispute resolution procedures, and how the *Supervisor* may be called upon during any dispute resolution.

</td></tr>
</table>

4.9.   Day-to-day procedures

The *Supervisor*'s day-to-day procedures include the following.

- Keeping track of the programme so as to prepare for tests/inspections and any marking required.
- Checking work done against the Works Information to notify any Defects found.
- Carrying out tests/inspections.
- Watching tests/inspections.
- Marking Equipment, Plant and Materials.
- Keeping track of risks which affect his activities.
- Keeping records of activities, for example a site diary (if required by the *Supervisor*'s personal contract).

4.9.1   Consequences of sign off

Clause 14.1 provides that the *Project Manager*'s or *Supervisor*'s acceptance of a communication from the *Contractor* or of his work does not change the *Contractor*'s responsibility to Provide the Works or his liability for his design. Therefore, the *Supervisor* does not give approval, but gives **acceptance** only – this acceptance does not relieve the *Contractor* of his responsibilities.

Example

The *Contractor* and *Supervisor* jointly inspect the *works*. The *Contractor* confirms in writing to the *Supervisor* the agreed finding of the inspection, which was that there were no problems or issues. The *Supervisor* acknowledges this communication. However, subsequent to the joint inspection of the *works* the *Supervisor* has noticed that there is a Defect in the *works* and he notifies the *Contractor* of a Defect.

The *Contractor* challenges the Defect by stating that the *Supervisor* had accepted the *works* on their joint inspection.

The *Supervisor* advises that his acceptance as identified in clause 14.1 of the *Contractor*'s *works* does not relieve the *Contractor* of his obligations under the contract and the notified Defect is valid.

Assumptions: (1) the Works Information requires an inspection at that point of progress in the *works*; (2) the Works Information requires the *Supervisor* and the *Contractor* to inspect the *works*, requires the *Contractor* to confirm the findings of the inspection in writing to the *Supervisor,* and requires the *Supervisor* to acknowledge the communication; and (3) the *Supervisor*'s personal contract includes for him to carry out the tasks required by the Works Information as well as the ECC.

4.10.   Defects

Defects in construction projects can be dangerous, costly and damaging to reputations, and inherent defects can lead to potential disaster, such as a tunnel collapse, building collapse or collapse of scaffolding.

Defects delay construction projects and rectifying poor workmanship or design wastes millions of pounds every year. Defects are also the major cause of dispute and construction litigation. The *Supervisor* will need to look out for Defects in the Plant and Materials being included in the *works* as well as in the *Contractor*'s workmanship, including unfinished or omitted work. The *Supervisor* may also be tasked with keeping an eye on what may be deficiencies in the Works Information; although these are not Defects as defined they may still affect the quality of the *works* or the performance of the *works* and the *Supervisor* is in a good position to assess improvements.

Notifying Defects is one of the most vital of the *Supervisor*'s daily activities and is essential for the achievement of quality objectives for the project. This section of the book describes how the *Supervisor* looks for and notifies Defects.

4.10.1   Identifying Defects

What the contract says
- Definition of a Defect (clause 11.2(5)).
- Definition of the Works Information (clause 11.2(19)) – referred to in the definition of a Defect.
- The Works Information is identified in the Contract Data.

(Appendix 7B details these clauses.)

What the contract doesn't say
The ECC does not describe how Defects are identified, nor does it describe what interactions the *Supervisor* must have with the *Contractor*, the *Employer* or the *Project Manager* for him to do his job properly.

What the Supervisor *does*
In order to identify Defects, the *Supervisor* must be familiar with the Works Information, both by the *Employer* and by the *Contractor*. The *Supervisor* must also be familiar with the legislation and regulations ('the applicable law') that apply to the *works*, whether listed in the Works Information or not. The *Supervisor* must set up communication channels with all the other parties working under the contract, and he must be on the Site regularly to be familiar with all aspects of the *works* and to compare the constructed *works* against the *Employer*'s requirements as described in the contract.

Actions for the *Supervisor*

- Identify Defects using the Works Information and the law applicable to the contract.
- Set up regular meetings with the *Project Manager* to discuss the *works*, the *Contractor*'s quality management system (QMS), the requirements of the contract and other matters about which the *Project Manager* wishes to be informed.
- Read and become familiar with the *Contractor*'s QMS.
- Access and file, where necessary, the method statements and risk assessments submitted by the *Contractor* to the *Project Manager* (but only if this is required by the Works Information).
- Find out how the *Project Manager* wishes the *Supervisor* to communicate any aspect of the *works* which the *Supervisor* considers to be incorrect but which is not contrary to the Works Information.
- Walk around the Site regularly to become familiar with the *works*, how the *Contractor* is interpreting the Works Information, and the QMS being applied by the *Contractor*.
- Regularly meet with the *Project Manager* to discuss the *works* and the *Project Manager*'s expectations with regard to being made aware of Defects.
- Make notes (including photos) about the *works* on a regular basis to provide a reference record of the progress of the *works* and whether new Defects are caused by other work. Record-keeping is discussed further in section 4.13.

4.10.2   Notifying Defects

What the contract says
- Definition of a Defect (clause 11.2(5)).
- A notification must be in writing (clause 13.1).
- To whom certificates are copied (clause 13.6).
- Notifications of a Defect are to be notified separately from other communications (clause 13.7).
- The *Contractor* and *Supervisor* notify Defects separately (clause 42.2).
- The *defects date* is identified in Contract Data part one.

(Appendix 7B details these clauses.)

In summary:

- Both the *Contractor* and the *Supervisor* are obliged to notify the other of a Defect 'as soon as he finds it'.
- Notifications are required to be
  - communicated and notified separately from other communications and
  - communicated in a form that can be read, copied and recorded.

Key message

Until the *defects date* the *Supervisor* and *Contractor* have an obligation to notify Defects as soon as they find them (clause 42.2).

What the contract doesn't say
Notifications are required to flow between the *Supervisor* and the *Contractor*; the contract does not require the *Project Manager* to be kept apprised of Defects or Defect notifications. The contract does not require the notification to include a period within which the Defect must be corrected. Separate notification for each Defect can be impractical in a large

project and the Parties may choose to agree a process that works for everyone, such as a weekly communication of Defects noticed in the preceding week, with provisos for more pressing Defects.

What the Supervisor *does*
Managing Defects entails much more than notifying Defects to the *Contractor* and receiving the *Contractor*'s notifications. The *Supervisor* has an opportunity to help the *Project Manager* keep abreast of the state of the *works* and the effectiveness of the *Contractor*'s QMS. If the *Project Manager* has not initiated the timetabling of meetings to discuss Defects with the *Supervisor,* and possibly the *Contractor*, then the *Supervisor* may choose to approach the *Project Manager* to request communications and meetings regarding Defects. At such meeting, Defects can be notified and discussed so that a joint way forward is agreed upon.

Actions for the Supervisor

- Devise a numbering method for the Defect notifications both from and to the *Supervisor*.
- Find out how the *Contractor* wants to be notified, for example, email or paper.
- Find out how the *Contractor*'s QMS requires notification of Defects to take place.
- Assess the effectiveness of the QMS and make adjustments as required (e.g. suggest changes to the *Project Manager*; make changes to his own systems to take account of any deficiencies in the *Contractor*'s system).
- Set up regular meetings with the *Project Manager*, either with or without the *Contractor*, to discuss notified Defects and Defects that have already been corrected or are to be corrected imminently.

4.10.3 Correcting Defects

What the contract says
- Definition of Completion (clause 11.2(2)).
- Tests/inspections may reveal a Defect (clause 40.4).
- The *Contractor* corrects Defects (clause 43.1).
- A Defect must be corrected in its *defect correction period* (clause 43.2).
- The *defect correction period* is identified in Contract Data part one.

(Appendix 7B details these clauses.)

Clause 43.1 obliges the *Contractor* to correct all Defects, whether notified by the *Contractor*, notified by the *Supervisor* or not notified at all. The contract draws a clear line about the correction of Defects notified before Completion and those notified after Completion. Defects notified before Completion are only required to be corrected at Completion, except for those which, by definition (Completion), need to be corrected to achieve Completion.

Clause 43.2 leaves the *Contractor* free to choose the timing of correcting a notified Defect up to Completion. This is sensible as the *Contractor* is in the best position to decide when to correct a notified Defect so as not to disrupt the *works*.

After Completion the *Contractor* has to correct notified Defects that were outstanding at Completion. Correction has to take place within the *defect correction period* (although Completion cannot be achieved if 'notified Defects' will prevent the *Employer* from using the *works* and prevent Others from doing their work (clause 11.2(2)).

What the contract doesn't say
The *Supervisor* has no described role regarding the correction of Defects. It is the *Contractor* who corrects Defects; the *Supervisor* has no say in when the correction happens or the circumstances surrounding the correction. The *Supervisor* cannot necessarily enforce Defect correction.

The contract does not detail what the *Supervisor* should do if he feels that the *defect correction period* should start immediately, regardless of whether the Defect will prevent Completion. The contract does not mention whether the *Supervisor* may make suggestions regarding the correction of Defects, and any transaction to accept a Defect takes place between the *Project Manager* and the *Contractor*.

The timescales for the correction of Defects are applicable to correcting a Defect revealed through a test/inspection, but the timing is not clear (see section 4.11). The timescale for correcting a Defect which has not been notified is not stated in the ECC, but there is no real need to as there are other safeguards in place (the definition of Completion and the overall requirement in clause 43.1 to correct a Defect).

What the Supervisor *does*
The *defect correction period* is stated in Contract Data part one and is therefore decided by the *Employer* in accordance with the length and complexity of the project. If Defects have been banded or categorised and a different *defect correction period* applies depending on the scale, type, area or criticality of the Defect, then the *Supervisor* will want to be specific in his Defect notification so that neither the *Contractor* nor the *Supervisor* can be in doubt about the length of time in which the *Contractor* must correct the Defect.

This is not to say that the *Supervisor* may not provide some leniency or practicality in his Defect notification. For example, if the *Supervisor* sees a cosmetic or otherwise non-critical Defect in a part of the Site where the *Contractor* is not currently working but is scheduled to work in a fortnight, then the *Supervisor* may, in his Defect notification, allow the *Contractor* to correct the Defect before the *Contractor* leaves that, second, part of the Site even though Contract Data part one, in accordance with the categorisation of the Defect, requires correction sooner.

Clause 43.2 requires the *Contractor* to correct at Completion all Defects which were notified before Completion. Alternatively, the correction of a Defect notified after Completion commences at the time when the Defect notification is made. Depending on the type of project, its length and complexity, the *Supervisor* may prefer that Defects are corrected throughout the course of the project, rather than only at Completion. However, the ECC does not support this unless the *Supervisor* can demonstrate that subsequent work would cover the Defect, or that Completion would not be achieved within the Accepted Programme if the Defect is not corrected before the *Contractor* progresses the *works*. Where the *Supervisor* is involved in the setting up of the project, this may be one of the areas where he may wish to ensure that he has good options when it comes to Defect correction.

If the *Supervisor* notifies a Defect, he is going to want to see its correction. He will want to keep a log of Defects notified by him and the *Contractor* and to tick them off as they have been corrected. (See the Defects log at Appendix 3D as an example of how to record Defects.) He will also report progress to the *Project Manager* so that the *Project Manager* has information about whether Defects will be corrected timeously so that Completion can take place on or before the Completion Date.

Actions for the *Supervisor*

- Understand whether any Option Z clauses provides for the *Supervisor* to dictate when Defect correction can take place.
- Be familiar with all the different *defect correction periods* in the Contract Data.
- Be sure to categorise each notified Defect in accordance with the Defect categories in the Contract Data.
- State in each Defect notification when the *defect correction period* for the Defect is to start.
- Be prepared to discuss Defect correction with the *Contractor*, especially where there are several methods of correction and the *Contractor* seeks advice on the least time-consuming or most effective method of correction.
- If the notification is about a Defect revealed through a test or inspection then include in the notification the requirement for the Defect to be corrected to continue with the *works* and any timescales to which the *Contractor* must adhere as extracted from the Accepted Programme.
- Keep a log of Defects, their notification and their correction.
- Keep the *Project Manager* informed of Defect correction, especially in the run up to the Completion Date, so that the *Project Manager* can assess whether any Defects will prevent Completion.
- Include Defect correction as an agenda item for the regular meeting about Defects held with the *Project Manager* (possibly including the *Contractor*).

More about the correction of Defects: Categories of Defects
Where categories of Defects are used to set different *defect correction periods*, the categories do not have to be described or added to clause 11.2 as definitions, as long as the mechanism of notification is clear. The following is an example of how different *defect correction periods* are identified in Contract Data part one.

4 Testing and Defects	■ The *defect correction period* is 2 weeks except that:
	  – the *defect correction period* for Defects notified as a Category A Defect is 8 hours
	  – the *defect correction period* for Defects notified as a Category B Defect is 2 days
	  – the *defect correction period* for Defects notified as a Category C Defect is 5 days.

4.10.4 Accepting Defects

What the contract says
- The procedure for accepting Defects is described in clauses 44.1 and 44.2.

(Appendix 7B details these clauses.)

What the contract doesn't say
There are no contractual actions for the *Supervisor*, even though it is likely that it was the *Supervisor* who notified the Defect in the first place and that it will be the *Supervisor* who will check any further work done by the *Contractor* to accept the Defect.

It is possible that the idea to accept a Defect may originate with the *Supervisor*, whether on Site with the *Contractor* or in regular discussions with the *Project Manager*. In any case, there is no doubt that the *Supervisor* can contribute positively to the described procedure to accept a Defect.

The *Project Manager* should advise the *Supervisor* of the change in the Works Information so that the *Supervisor* can monitor the work done with reference to the Works Information. The *Supervisor* should also be made aware of any change to the Completion Date (and, therefore, potentially Completion) since clause 43.2 requires the *defect correction period* of Defects notified before Completion to begin at Completion.

What the Supervisor *does*
Although the *Supervisor* is not required to act under this clause, he should ask the *Project Manager* to inform him of and make him party to any discussions about accepting a Defect. See section 5.3.4.

Actions for the *Supervisor*

- Ensure that accepting Defects is an agenda item for the regular meeting about Defects held with the *Project Manager*.
- Communicate with the *Contractor* so that he [the *Supervisor*] is aware of (1) any accepted Defects where the appropriate communication with the *Project Manager* has not taken place, and (2) any change to the Completion Date.
- Suggest to the *Project Manager* that a Defect should be accepted, where this is appropriate.
- Keep track of any accepted Defects, especially where they impact on other parts of the *works*.

4.10.5 Uncorrected Defects

What the contract says
- The procedure for accepting Defects where the *Contractor* does not/cannot correct a Defect within its *defect correction period* (clause 45.1 and 45.2).

(Appendix 7B details this clause.)

This clause may be required before Completion; however, this book deals with uncorrected Defects in section 5.

4.10.6 Searching for Defects

What the contract says
- The procedure for searching for Defects (clause 42.1).

(Appendix 7B details this clause.)

Clause 42.1 allows the *Supervisor* to instruct the *Contractor* to search for a Defect. The clause describes what 'searching' means and things that the *Contractor* may need to provide for the test to be carried out. The clause requires the *Supervisor* to provide reasons for his instruction, but does not restrict the type of reasons. Clause 60.1(10) provides that an instructed search which does not yield a Defect is a compensation event unless the search is required only because the *Contractor* did not give sufficient notice that he was going to do work that would cover a required test/inspection (section 4.7 discusses this compensation event in more detail).

What the Supervisor *does*
Searching for a Defect and any resulting notification of a Defect requires the *Supervisor* to interact with the *Project Manager* and the *Contractor*. The *Supervisor* also undertakes the activities required by clause 42.1 and any subsequent activities under clauses 42.2 and 43.2 as well as compensation event clause 60.1(10).

Actions for the *Supervisor*

- Advise the *Project Manager* that he [the *Supervisor*] intends to instruct the *Contractor* to undertake a search for a Defect, providing reasons and his forecast of any impact on the programme and budget of the project.
- Discuss the forthcoming instruction and his requirements about the search with the *Contractor*.
- Instruct the *Contractor* to undertake the search and instruct any required activities to support the search, for example, provide materials, uncover a part of the *works* or undertake a specific test which is not required by the Works Information.
- Be on Site to watch the search, for example, the uncovering of work and carrying out of a test.
- Record the search, including all activities before and after the search.
- Advise the *Project Manager* of the results of the search, especially if no Defect is found and the *Contractor* was not inefficient in his notifications for a test and a compensation event could therefore arise.
- Notify any Defect and provide comments about when correction should take place.
- Provide the *Project Manager* with information about the Defect and its impact on the rest of the *works*, including the programme.

4.11. Tests and inspections

What the contract says
- Compensation event if the *Employer* does not provide something he is required to (clause 60.1(3)).
- Compensation event if the *Employer* does not provide things for tests and inspections as he is required to (clause 60.1(16)).
- Full details of how tests/inspections are carried out (clauses 40.1 to 40.6).
- Testing/inspection of Plant and Materials (clause 41.1).

(Appendix 7B details these clauses.)

What the contract doesn't say
There is no ECC contractual obligation on the *Supervisor* or the *Project Manager* to advise the *Employer* to get ready the things that the Works Information said would be provided by the *Employer*. However, this may be included in the *Supervisor*'s personal contract.

There is no contractual requirement to keep the *Project Manager* in the loop about tests/inspections, even though they could affect the parts of the project for which the *Project Manager* is responsible. This may affect the *Project Manager*'s assessment of the cost of repeating a test/inspection to be paid by the *Contractor*.

There is no mention of the *Contractor*'s right to watch tests or inspections carried out by the *Supervisor*, although he will be notified that they are going to take place and afterwards he will be notified of the results. However, in the spirit of mutual trust and co-operation, there is no reason why the *Supervisor* would stop the *Contractor* from observing.

There are no timescales for the correction of a Defect revealed by a test/inspection. As Completion cannot be achieved unless Defects preventing the *Employer* from using the *works* are corrected, the ECC user can infer that the *Contractor* must correct the Defect revealed by the test/inspection if the Defect would prevent the *Employer* using the *works* (or Others from doing their work – clause 11.2(2)).

There is no definition of 'unnecessary', where the *Supervisor* may cause unnecessary delay in carrying out his test/inspection. The interpretation will be left to the *Project Manager* if the *Contractor* notifies a compensation event under clause 60.1(11). A delay in carrying out a test/inspection that could lead to a payment to the *Contractor* is discussed in section 4.7. Both of these issues may be addressed in the *Supervisor*'s personal contract.

There is no mention of checking measurements, which may not be necessary in many contracts. It is the *Project Manager* who is responsible for assessments in section 5 of the core clauses and so it may be that measurement checks are part of the *Project Manager*'s remit.

What the Supervisor *does*
It is best for all parties and for the project if the *Supervisor* communicates with the *Project Manager* about tests/inspections; the *Employer* is advised to ensure that the *Supervisor*'s personal contract facilitates this. Preparing for, carrying out and reporting on tests/inspections by the *Supervisor* can be vital in some contracts (e.g. process contracts) and involvement is required by the *Supervisor*, the *Project Manager*, the *Contractor* and the *Employer*. It makes sense that it is the *Supervisor* who pulls things together and coordinates requirements.

Actions for the *Supervisor*

- Make sure that the tests and inspections included in the Works Information and the applicable law provide enough information to assess the *works*. If the *Supervisor* thinks that more or different tests need to be done, he may choose to approach the *Employer* and the *Project Manager* for further discussions.
- Ask the *Project Manager* if there are other tests/inspections that he would recommend. Take action as required.
- Ask the *Project Manager* if there are tests/inspections in which he is particularly interested. Take action as required.
- Be aware of upcoming tests/inspections and whether the *Employer* is to provide anything for the test/inspection.
- Ask the *Project Manager* if he is going to notify the *Employer* that facilities etc. are required soon. If not, the *Supervisor* should do so (and this action may be required of him in his personal contract).
- Keep records of all tests/inspections, their outcome, facilities provided and any known costs of taking or repeating tests.
- Notify the *Contractor* before the *Supervisor* carries out tests/inspections, making sure that enough notice is given to the *Contractor* so that he can prepare for it.
- Ask the *Contractor* if he wants to watch the test and provide access for him (if required).
- Carry out the test/inspection.
- Make sure not to take too long to prepare for and carry out the tests/inspections and potentially delay the *Contractor* unnecessarily, especially where the success of the test will trigger a payment to the *Contractor*.
- Notify the *Contractor* of the results of the tests/inspections.
- If the test/inspection shows a Defect, make the notification and ask the *Contractor* what his timescales are to correct the Defect so that the *Supervisor* can schedule another test/inspection. Advise the *Project Manager* of the Defect, especially if the test is on the critical path of the Accepted Programme and/or a Key Date. Be a part of any discussions to accept the Defect.
- If the test/inspection fails a second time, hold dialogue with the *Contractor* and the *Project Manager* regarding forecasts and predictions of future tests etc.
- Receive notification of any tests/inspections to be carried out by the *Contractor*. Make sure that the *Contractor* has given enough notice; advise the *Contractor* that more time is required if this is the case.
- Receive notification of the results of the *Contractor*'s tests/inspections. Take action if the results do not tally with the *Supervisor*'s assessment.
- Make sure that the *Supervisor* is aware of when all the *Contractor*'s tests will take place and what is required to carry them out.
- Watch any test carried out by the *Contractor*, as long as the test is required by the Works Information and the applicable law. Otherwise, ask the *Contractor* if the *Supervisor* may watch the test and any inspections the *Contractor* plans to carry out.
- Contribute to the *Project Manager*'s assessment of the cost of repeating a test/inspection after a Defect, where the *Project Manager* has asked the *Supervisor* to contribute.
- Ask the *Contractor* to tell the *Supervisor* when he needs Plant and Materials which the Works Information requires to be tested so that the *Supervisor* can undertake the tests timeously (the *Supervisor* should be fully aware of the Accepted Programme so that he can still do the tests timeously even if the *Contractor* does not give him notice).
- Tell the *Project Manager* that the Plant and Materials have passed their tests and so can be brought to the Working Areas.

4.12. Marking

Marking is not required on all contracts. When it is required it is unlikely to be the most vital part of the contract, but it is helpful to the *Project Manager* if the *Supervisor* oversees this requirement. In general, the *Supervisor* will be on Site anyway and it will be simple to fit these actions into his daily routine.

What the contract says
- The procedures for marking Plant and Materials (clause 70.1).
- The procedure for marking Equipment, Plant and Materials (clause 71.1).

(Appendix 7B details these clauses.)

What the contract doesn't say
Communications are not covered by the ECC. The *Supervisor*'s personal contract may include further requirements.

What the Supervisor *does*
The *Supervisor*'s obligations under these clauses are very simple. Apart from communications with the *Contractor* and the *Project Manager*, there are no added requirements. There are no contractual consequences of the *Supervisor* not carrying out his duties unless they are included as an *Employer*'s risk and a clause 60.1(14) compensation event is notified.

Actions for the *Supervisor*

- Check the Works Information to see if there are any requirements for the *Contractor* to prepare any Equipment, Plant and Materials outside the Working Areas for marking.
- Access the Accepted Programme and check whether the requirement to prepare for marking any Equipment, Plant and Materials is included as an operation, date or procedure or a Condition for a Key Date (Key Dates will also be in the Contract Data). Alternatively, check when the Accepted Programme shows the Equipment, Plant and Materials to be required (perhaps as 'Equipment or other resources') or ask the *Contractor* what his timetable is.
- Access the Contract Data for a description of the Working Areas as the *Supervisor* may need to travel to another part of the country or in some instances overseas to carry out the marking. The *Supervisor* may also need to access the Works Information by the *Contractor* or the *Contractor*'s tender and he may need to speak with the *Contractor* to understand more about the locations of any Equipment, Plant and Materials which are outside the Working Areas.
- Advise the *Project Manager* that he [the *Supervisor*] will shortly be carrying out the marking of items as required.
- Carry out the marking of the required items.
- Take photographs and make notes as required as evidence that this obligation is complete and the *Employer*'s interests are protected.
- Advise the *Project Manager* that the marking is complete so that the *Project Manager* can continue to manage the programme.

4.13. Records

What the contract says/doesn't say
There are no references in the ECC that tie the *Supervisor* to the keeping of records. There are a couple of places in the contract where it would obviously benefit the *Supervisor* to have knowledge of events easily to hand, such as a list of Defects or a list of items marked under clauses 70.1 and 71.1, but the keeping of a site diary and other records are not the obligations of a *Supervisor* under the ECC.

In fact, there are a number of clauses where the keeping of records would fall more naturally to the *Project Manager*, for example weather in clause 60.1(13) and resources used on Site in clause 31.2 (penultimate bullet point).

Key message

If the *Employer* wants the *Supervisor* to keep records then that obligation should be included in the *Supervisor*'s personal contract.

The *Supervisor* does not have the same duties as a traditional clerk of works. There is no contractual requirement for the *Supervisor* to keep records. The *Employer* and the *Project Manager* should both be aware of this and take appropriate action to ensure that site records are made for each project.

What the Supervisor *does*
If the person appointed to the post of *Supervisor* in an ECC contract is used to the role of a clerk of works and is used to maintaining records, then it may be that he will simply absorb the role of record-keeper as part of his daily duties. If the *Supervisor* realises that his personal contract does not include for the role of record-keeper, then he can take steps to alert the *Employer*, who can then do what he needs to do to alter the situation.

Actions for the *Supervisor*

- Ascertain whether his personal contract requires him to keep records on the Site.
- If not, approach the *Employer* and the *Project Manager* to ascertain whether the *Project Manager* or another person will keep records.
- Recognising that record-keeping is good project management, consider offering to keep records.
- Draw up the format for records, such as the site diary, to facilitate active recording.

This section on record-keeping is based on the assumption that it is the *Supervisor* who keeps the records, but bear in mind that some of this responsibility may fall to the *Project Manager* or someone else in a particular contract.

Record the facts of all on-site activities and events and everything that happens in and around the construction Site clearly and concisely.

4.13.1   Record-keeping

The importance of site notebooks and the recording of all events cannot be overemphasised: these records facilitate forensic analysis and provide contemporaneous evidence of the project which can be used by the *Employer* and, if needed, the *Adjudicator* and a *tribunal*. Every member of the Site supervisory staff should keep a daily site notebook in which is recorded everything of any importance that he has done or seen that day. There is no need to write extensively, but the notes should be accurate and objective, and they should be sufficient to be of value when consulted about a particular item at a later date – perhaps many months later.

The *Supervisor* should ensure (and check at regular intervals) that each assistant continues to keep a daily site notebook. To cover longer-term events, a wallchart (as shown in Table 4.2) should be posted showing important contract dates for necessary action (to be reviewed monthly). This chart could include:

- when the *Employer* requires information regarding the payment of *delay damages*
- dates for inspections before the expiry of any maintenance period
- when to request the extension of a bond or insurance validity (including that of vehicles used by the *Supervisor*'s staff).

Table 4.2 Time wallchart

Item reference	Time data	Comments
1	*starting date*	
2	*access date(s)*	
3	Key Dates	
4	Sectional Completion Date(s)	
5	*completion date*	
6	*defects date*	
7	*defect correction period*	

During his daily checks and activities, the *Supervisor* will come into contact with almost all the people working on the project, including Subcontractors, building control officers and consultants. The *Supervisor* therefore has the opportunity to be fully aware of what is happening on Site, to anticipate problems and suggest workarounds or solutions – but to put this into effect, his personal contract must require him to do these things.

4.13.2   Site diary

The *Supervisor* should ensure that a site diary (Table 4.3) is kept, recording all the work achieved by the *Contractor* each day and any notable events, as well as the project title, date, file reference and contract reference. Progress photos and drawings should also be kept and referenced where applicable. An example is included in Figure 4.3.

Figure 4.3 Marked up drawing showing the progress of the *works* (Figure by Barry Trebes)

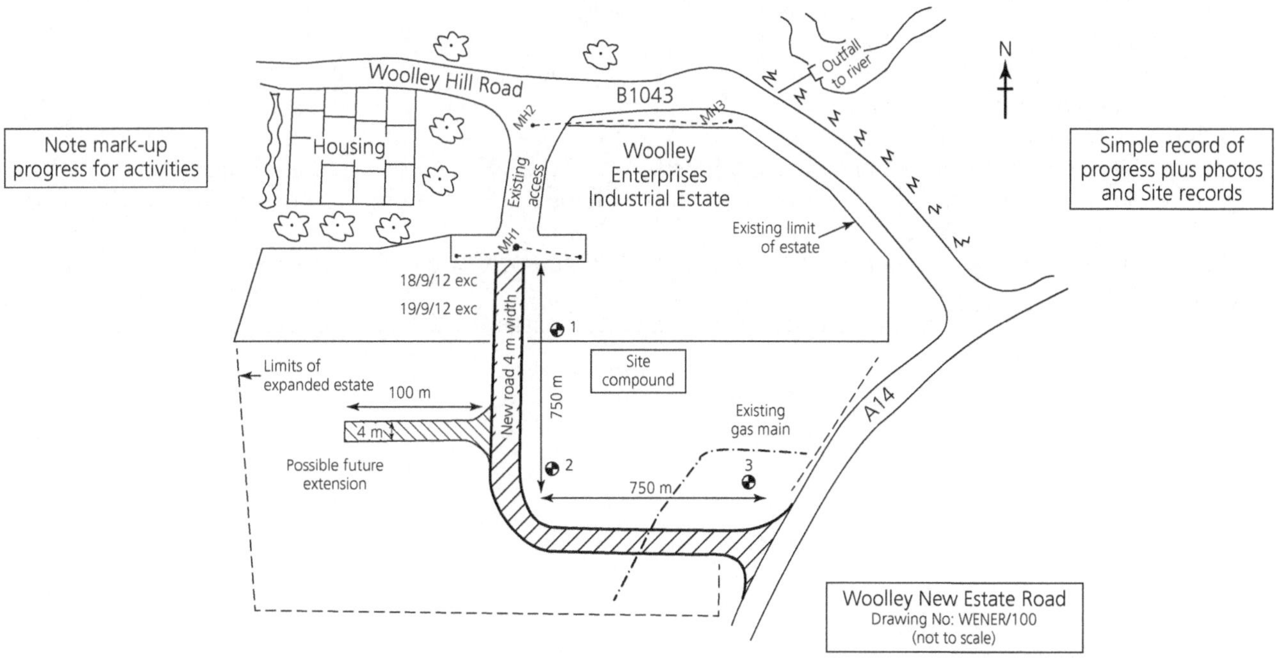

Examples of notable events include the following:

- works in progress
- important construction events, such as concrete pouring
- Site directions
- personnel resources used
- Plant and Materials delivered
- items removed from Site
- storage
- movement of Equipment
- underground services
- time lost and why
- tests and inspections carried out
- major Defects and rectification
- delays
- weather conditions
- accidents
- visitors
- remarks.

These records can also anticipate events, record conversations and suggestions, and note deviations that are not Defects but which may cause problems in the future.

One of the most important areas for record-keeping is where work will be covered up, such as the routing of pipes or cables, for which a programme of progressive inspection may be necessary.

Any records to be completed by the *Contractor* and submitted to the *Supervisor* should be detailed in the Works Information (e.g. weekly labour returns) and any duties or actions required by the *Supervisor* should be detailed in his personal contract.

> **Site diary tips**
>
> - Entries should be clear and concise.
> - Entries should be written so that they will make sense when read in several months' time.
> - The diary should not be loose-leaf.
> - Each day's entries should follow each other – no gaps.
> - Afterthoughts should be written in or referred to in the margin and dated at the time of the entry.
> - All meetings and telephone calls, however informal, should be recorded, along with conclusions reached and instructions given and received.
> - The *Supervisor* should ensure and should check at regular intervals that each assistant continues to keep a daily site diary.

4.13.3 Translation of the *Supervisor*'s site diaries into commercial/planning activities

Table 4.3 The *Supervisor*'s site diary

Example of the type of information to be recorded (in no particular order)	Information source	Interface with Commercial					
		Early warnings	Quotations for compensation events	*Project Manager's* instructions	Defined Cost	Disallowable Cost	Insurances
Weather ■ *weather measurements*	Contract Data part one	✓	✓	✓			
Progress	Works Information	✓	✓	✓	✓	✓	
Incidents on Site ■ industrial disputes		✓	✓	✓	✓	✓	✓
Compensation events	Core clause 6 list of compensation events – secondary options	✓	✓	✓	✓	✓	✓
Insurance matters	Conditions of contract – insurance procedures	✓					✓
Delays and disruption ■ operational issues ■ *Contractor's* plant breakdowns ■ access		✓	✓	✓	✓	✓	✓
Programme: activities on Site ■ planned ■ actual ■ Key Dates ■ sectional dates ■ site hours	Works Information Accepted Programme	✓	✓	✓	✓	✓	
People (labour on Site)		✓	✓	✓	✓	✓	
Equipment on Site ■ Equipment breakdowns ■ Equipment not required for the *works*		✓	✓	✓	✓	✓	
Plant and Materials on Site ■ Plant and Materials not required for the *works*		✓	✓	✓	✓	✓	
Health and safety		✓		✓			
Environment		✓		✓			
Security	Works Information	✓		✓			✓
Public		✓		✓			
Quality	Quality inspections Testing plans	✓	✓	✓	✓	✓	

Table 4.3 Continued

Example of the type of information to be recorded (in no particular order)	Information source	Early warnings	Quotations for compensation events	*Project Manager*'s instructions	Defined Cost	Disallowable Cost	Insurances
		Interface with Commercial					
Ground conditions	Site Information	✓	✓	✓	✓	✓	
Defects ■ notify ■ search		✓		✓			
Tests and inspections	Works Information – quality inspections and testing plans	✓		✓			
Supervisor's tests and inspections	Works Information	✓		✓			
Subcontractors		✓		✓			
Suppliers		✓		✓			
Others		✓		✓			
Employer		✓		✓			
Damage to the *works*		✓					✓
Risk Register		✓					

4.14. In practice

The ECC describes the procedures that direct the actions of those working on the project to fulfil the rights and obligation of the Parties. However, there will always be issues on a project that are not directly related to the contract and the *Supervisor* may need some clarification with regards to his actions on the project. Table 4.4 discusses examples of questions that may be asked by a *Supervisor* who is experienced on other forms of contract.

Table 4.4 Points of clarification that may be needed by the *Supervisor*

Point of clarification	Commentary
What does acceptance mean? Am I putting the *Employer* at risk if I don't pick up a Defect in the design?	The *Project Manager*'s or the *Supervisor*'s acceptance of a communication or of his *works* does not change the *Contractor*'s responsibility to Provide the Works or his liability for his design (clause 14.1). The *Employer*'s risk will increase because even if the fault is caught prior to use, the performance of the *works* may be affected, and correction of any fault takes time and increases costs (of supervision etc.). However, the *Contractor*'s liability is not negated or reduced if a Defect is not identified.
What is a Defect?	ECC provides an objective and measurable test of a Defect in clause 11.2(5). The *Supervisor* must understand that work which he regards as defective may not in fact be a Defect as defined.

Table 4.4 Continued

Point of clarification	Commentary
Verbal instructions	Verbal instructions are not recognised in the ECC – clause 13 provides rules about communications.
Daywork sheets	This terminology is not used or recognised in the ECC.
Uncooperative people – *Contractor*	If a member of the *Contractor*'s team is being unhelpful, obstructive or difficult then the *Supervisor* should inform the *Project Manager* as it is the *Project Manager* who has the right to remove people from Site.
When are activities complete?	An activity is complete when the activity is without Defects which would delay or be covered by immediately following work. The *Supervisor* does not make the decision about Completion, but his opinion may be valued by the *Project Manager*.
Is the *Contractor*'s non-conformance system the same as a Defect?	The *Contractor*'s non-conformance system, perhaps as part of his wider QMS, may be suitable and may mirror the actions required by the ECC. However, the ECC is very precise about what is considered to be a Defect and this definition is the one which will take precedence in the case of a differing opinion between the ECC and the *Contractor*'s QMS. (Section 2.2 provides more information on a *Contractor*'s QMS.)
Do I have to notify each Defect separately or can I group them together in one notification?	The ECC requires the notification for each Defect to be separate. In larger, more complex projects, the parties may decide to work from a weekly Defect notice, or some other way that helps the parties work together. The danger with grouping together a number of Defects onto one notification is that the individual Defects might not be sufficiently visible. An individual Defect might be of minor importance, but it could lead to complications if it is overlooked or not actioned.
Is the *Contractor*'s failure to follow his own quality plan a Defect?	If the *Contractor*'s quality plan is a part of the Works Information, then a deviation could be construed as a Defect. However, it is unlikely that this part of the *Contractor*'s tender will be called Works Information.
Do I have to stick with the *period for reply*?	The *Supervisor* is required to reply within the period indicated in the *period for reply* in the Contract Data or any other periods contained in the Works Information for certain matters, for example, design acceptance process, tests and inspections. If he needs more time, there is nothing to stop him approaching the *Contractor*, explaining the situation and agreeing a different timescale.
What happens if I am late or slow in replying to a communication from the *Contractor*?	A late response is a compensation event under clause 60.1(6). However the *Contractor* would still have to demonstrate under clause 61.4 that the late response has had an effect on Defined Cost, Completion or meeting a Key Date. It is better for the *Supervisor* to discuss the matter with the *Contractor* before the time expires.

Table 4.4 Continued

Point of clarification	Commentary
The *Project Manager* ignores my advice. The *Project Manager* is putting pressure on me to take actions that I feel uncomfortable with as the *Supervisor*. What can I do?	The *Supervisor* is independent of the *Project Manager* and reports to the *Employer* rather than the *Project Manager*. As the *Supervisor*, you have a clearly defined role in the contract and you are responsible to the *Employer* for the quality of the *works* as described in the Works Information. If the *Project Manager* chooses to ignore advice you have given in good faith then you have no further remit under the ECC. You may choose to inform the *Employer*, especially where you are on a personal contract and your actions are being measured. Being put under pressure by the *Project Manager* is unpleasant. However, the *Supervisor* must fulfil his obligations under the contract and for the contract to work optimally, the *Supervisor* must do what he is required to do. If you are uncomfortable with the pressure being imposed by the *Project Manager* then you may choose to advise the *Employer*.
What powers do I have?	The *Supervisor* may give instructions (clause 27.3) and can issue an instruction to search for a Defect (clause 42.1). Other responsibilities focus on notifications. The *Supervisor* has no powers to agree or change the Works Information. If the *Supervisor* feels that work is defective or not of good quality but is acceptable against the Works Information, then the *Supervisor* could bring this to the attention of the *Employer* and the *Project Manager* first. Although the *Supervisor* may give an instruction to the *Contractor*, the *Contractor* is only required to obey the instruction if it is given in accordance with the contract.
What if the Works Information is silent on the quality of the *works*?	The *Supervisor* is not responsible for the quality of the *works*. The *Supervisor*'s job is to check that the *works* represent the specifications and other standards included in the Works Information. It is unlikely that the Works Information will have absolutely no information on specifications, guidance and policies; however, if there is no detail in the Works Information, then the standards required by the legislation applicable to the *works* in the relevant country will apply.
I usually like to let the *Contractor* know who is boss on day one by making him take down or rebuild his first bit of work.	This attitude is contrary to the ECC's requirement to foster mutual trust and co-operation (clause 10.1) and may therefore be regarded by some as a breach of contract. Any instruction given by the *Supervisor* to the *Contractor* must be obeyed. But the *Contractor* may then notify a compensation event to the *Project Manager* where the *Supervisor*'s instruction requires an action that differs from the Works Information. The *Project Manager* can only approach the *Supervisor* directly if it is allowed for in his personal contract and in the personal contract of the *Supervisor*. Otherwise, the *Project Manager* may need to inform the *Employer*, who may then choose to take action against the *Supervisor*.

Table 4.4 Continued

Point of clarification	Commentary
When should I start to manage Defects? At Completion?	Defects should be notified by the *Contractor* and the *Supervisor* to each other 'as soon as he finds it'. The timetable for the correction of Defects depends on the *Contractor*'s programme, the *defect correction period* and any changes to clause 43.2. Defects should be managed from the start of the contract, but there could be more focus on correcting Defects in the weeks just after Completion.
When does my involvement end?	The *Supervisor* is required to issue the Defects Certificate, which is issued around the *defects date*, usually 52 weeks after Completion (but perhaps 104 weeks for process plant projects). The *Supervisor*'s involvement therefore ends approximately a year after Completion, depending on the end of the last *defect correction period*.
If the *Contractor* doesn't have to start correcting the Defect until Completion, why should I notify a Defect as soon as I see it?	Active management of Defects means it is always better to keep track of what is going on at the Site. Pre-Completion, the *Contractor* is in the best position to decide when a Defect should be corrected. In deciding when to correct a Defect the *Contractor* will take into consideration how it can be remedied with the least impact on the *works* being constructed.
Can I tell the *Contractor* what I think is the best way to fix the Defect?	The *Supervisor* is there to ensure that the *works* are constructed in accordance with the Works Information and the applicable law. It is not the *Supervisor*'s role to direct the *Contractor* in how he should correct a Defect.
There is a part of the Works Information that I think is wrong. What happens if I tell the *Contractor* to do something differently?	The *Supervisor* may not change the Works Information or any other part of the contract.
I am not going to be able to respond to a TQA in time. What can I do? (Note that a Technical Query and Answer (TQA) is not recognised as being part of the ECC.)	The most obvious response is that the *Supervisor* should talk to the *Contractor* and state that he cannot respond and ask for more time. It is unlikely that the *Contractor* will refuse him the time; but the delay may affect other work and the *Contractor* should inform the *Supervisor* of this so that decisions are made co-operatively and knowingly of the consequences. ECC does not allow the *Supervisor* to extend the *period for reply* but there are no real consequences if it is the *Supervisor* who proactively extends a *period for reply* which affects only him (and does not, for example, cause a Key Date to be missed). The *Supervisor* is nevertheless advised to inform the *Project Manager* of the events in case the Risk Register is affected.
I am the *Supervisor* on a Site with several contractors whose work inter-relates and overlaps with each other. The *Employer* wishes to take partial possession of some areas of the *works*. What should I look out for?	The *Supervisor* may wish to consider the following: ■ other contractors causing damage to the work of the *Contractor* ■ potential arguments about the cause of a Defect – use by other contractors, use and/or misuse by *Employer*'s own staff ■ repairs to the *works* ■ damage to the *works*/insurance matters ■ health and safety requirements, as stated in the Works Information (the *Project Manager* is responsible for general health and safety matters).

Table 4.4 Continued

Point of clarification	Commentary
I am used to a contractor producing a schedule of information, listing what he will need and when. I can't find this in the ECC.	The Accepted Programme will provide details of the order and timing of the work of the *Employer* and Others (Others could include a design team, where the Works Information and Contract Data allows for this) and it may be that a schedule of information can be extracted from the Accepted Programme. Otherwise, any requirement of the *Contractor* to produce a list of drawings that he will provide and when must be stated in the Works Information.
Do I still have to check drawings for inconsistencies?	Under the ECC, the *Supervisor* must check the *works* against the Works Information and the law. He is not required to check drawings being provided to the *Contractor* for inconsistencies between drawings and/or the Works Information (although this may be part of his personal contract with the *Employer*). Nor is he required to check drawings provided by the *Contractor* unless the Works Information requires the *Contractor* to submit drawings to the *Supervisor* for checking.
The *Contractor* is not giving me access to his construction health and safety plan. Can I instruct him to give me access?	ECC does not require the *Supervisor* to monitor the health and safety plan and the *Supervisor* can only notify a Defect if it is a part of the *works* that is not in accordance with the health and safety required by the law or the Works Information. However, the Works Information may require the *Contractor* to provide his health and safety plan to the *Supervisor* and may require the *Supervisor* to monitor the *Contractor*'s compliance.
The structural consultant has reported me to the *Project Manager* because he instructed me to check the tolerances of the steelwork which arrived on Site but I had to be at another part of the Site to undertake a pressure test. Should I have postponed the test to fit in with the structural consultant's instruction?	There are three things to bear in mind in answering this question: ■ *Is the Supervisor required to obey instructions from the structural consultant?* In the ECC, the *Supervisor* reports only to the *Employer*; however, the Works Information or the *Supervisor*'s personal contract may require the *Supervisor* to work with the structural consultant. Further, unless the *Supervisor*'s personal contract requires the *Supervisor* to obey the *Project Manager*, the *Supervisor*'s being reported to the *Project Manager* will not close the issue. ■ *Is the Contractor allowed to deliver those materials to the Site at that time?* The Works Information may provide constraints on how and when the *Contractor* may deliver materials to the Site or the Working Areas. ■ *Does the Works Information or the law require the Contractor or the Supervisor to test/inspect the steelwork?* The Works Information may direct the *Contractor* not to deliver the steelwork until it has been inspected by the *Supervisor*; or it may require the *Supervisor* to inspect the steelwork on arrival; or it may not mention inspection at all. It is only if the *Supervisor* was required to inspect the steelwork precisely on arrival that the *Supervisor* may be accused of neglecting his duties. In reality, there are many scenarios in which the *Supervisor* could be doing something else: the pressure test was a repeat test and so not on the original testing schedule; the delivery of the steelwork was not on the critical path and so the *Supervisor* had some leeway; or the steelwork had been delivered early and the inspection was not scheduled until the following week.

Table 4.4 Continued

Point of clarification	Commentary
I would normally check reinforcement positions but the *Contractor* says I don't have to. Should I do it anyway?	If the Works Information or the law requires the reinforcement positions to be inspected, then the *Supervisor* is required to do it. If only a simple check is required, rather than a test/inspection, then the *Supervisor*'s duty to do this can only come from his personal contract.

4.14.1 The *Contractor*'s QMS

It is likely that the Works Information of an ECC contract will require some sort of quality system from the *Contractor*. This may be as simple as a requirement for the *Contractor* to provide evidence of certification with a nationwide body; for example, the *Contractor* must have an up-to-date ISO 9001 certificate during the period of the contract and up to the *defects date* and must adhere to the requirements of ISO 9001. Alternatively, it may be an acceptance of the QMS that the *Contractor* submitted as required at tender stage and which was evaluated as part of the technical evaluation. Some smaller projects may simply rely on the *Supervisor*'s Defect notification system. However, the *Supervisor* is not responsible for the undefined quality of the *works*.

Part of the *Supervisor*'s job is to note any differences between the Works Information and the *works*. To do this the *Supervisor* relies on the definition of the *works* and the content of the Works Information. If the *Contractor* does not adhere to a part of his QMS but this does not impact on the *works* as built, this will not be a Defect. However, if the Works Information or an Option Z clause states that a non-conformance with the accepted QMS or required ISO 9001 will be regarded as a Defect and will require immediate rectification, then the *Supervisor* has more scope to compare the *Contractor*'s QMS as required with the way it is being applied on the Site. Therefore, the *Contractor* recording a non-compliance in his own QMS is not the same thing as it being notified as a Defect under the contract.

The active management of Defects is an essential part of the project management process and proactive communications should be made by all parties on Site.

Section 5

NEC3: The Role of the *Supervisor*
ISBN 978-0-7277-6096-8

From Completion to the *defects date*

(Note that most of the comments about Completion can also refer to Completion of a *section* of the *works*.)

This is the last phase of the project. It covers the period of time after Completion has been reached until the end of the period of time (commonly 52 weeks) during which the *Contractor* is still required to correct Defects (Figure 5.1).

Figure 5.1 Completion to the *defects date*

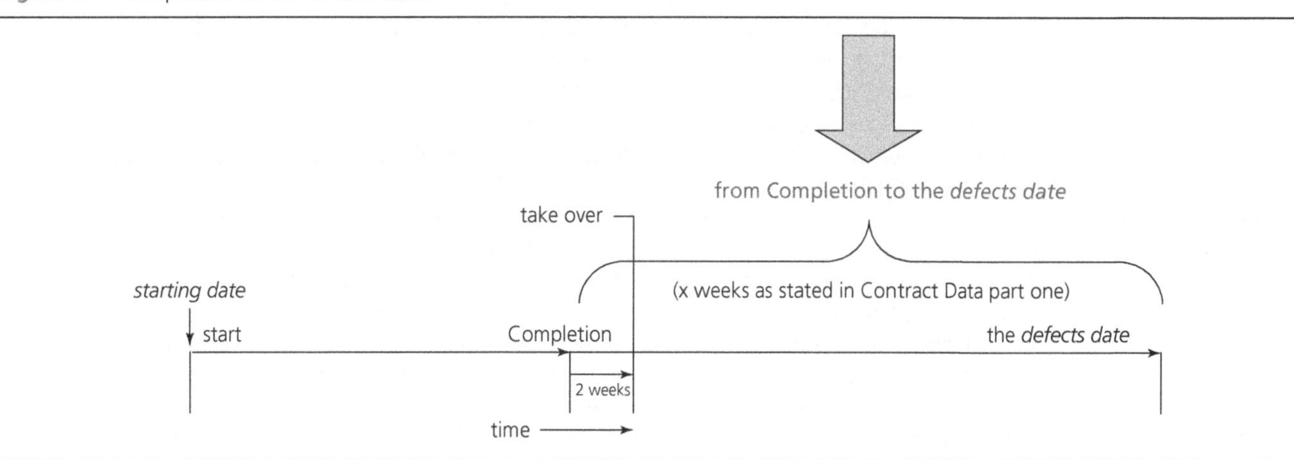

The following terms are used in this section, and are explained further in Table 5.1:

- planned Completion
- Completion
- Completion Date
- *completion date*
- date of Completion
- take over
- Defects
- Defects Certificate
- *defect correction period*.

Unlike other forms of contract, the ECC does not allow for 'practical completion'. In the ECC, Completion is a binary decision – either Completion has been achieved, or it has not been achieved. The *Project Manager*'s decision about whether Completion has been reached has the potential to be objective, depending on how Completion has been described in the Works Information and how the Works Information describes what must be done for the *Employer* and Others to start using the *works*.

5.1.   Understanding the terms

Table 5.1 Understanding the terms from Completion to the *defects date*

planned Completion	■ planned Completion is the date included by the *Contractor* on the programme that he submits to the *Project Manager* for acceptance and is therefore likely to appear on the Accepted Programme. ■ It represents the date on which the *Contractor* is planning to reach Completion. It can therefore be a date prior to the Completion Date or the same date as the Completion Date. ■ Any period of time between the date of planned Completion and the Completion Date is terminal float, which belongs to the *Contractor*. ■ If a compensation event pushes the Completion Date further on, then the *Contractor* can change his date of planned Completion by the same number of days.
Completion	■ Completion is a defined term; it is also a status rather than a point in time. ■ The Completion Date and planned Completion are dates in the Accepted Programme, but reaching the programmed date does not automatically mean that Completion has taken place. ■ Completion can take place on the Completion Date or before the Completion Date or after the Completion Date. ■ The *Project Manager* decides when Completion takes place. ■ Completion (as defined) is when the *Contractor* has done all the work which the Works Information says he must do in order to achieve Completion and has corrected Defects that would prevent the use of the *works*. Therefore: – the Works Information should state what needs to be done in order to reach Completion – the *Project Manager* must be able to decide whether the necessary Defects have been corrected or not.
Completion Date	■ The Completion Date is on the Accepted Programme. ■ It is based on the *completion date* which is included in the Contract Data, but it may change through accepted compensation events. ■ The Completion Date is a target date to achieve. There may be damages for Completion being achieved at a later date and/or a bonus for early Completion.
completion date	■ The *completion date* is identified in the Contract Data. It will be the same as the Completion Date if a compensation event has not changed the date. ■ It is the date on which the parties expect Completion to be achieved.
date of Completion	■ The date of Completion is the date on which the *Project Manager* decides Completion has taken place. ■ The date of Completion may be on the Completion Date or on another date.
take over	■ The *Employer* can take over the *works* up to two weeks after Completion. ■ The *Employer* may choose to take over the *works* early if (1) Contract Data part one does not state that he is not willing to do so, and (2) the *works* are available early. ■ Take over affects the *Contractor*'s access to the *works* for the purposes of correcting Defects.
Defects	■ Defect is a defined term. It has two strands: – work which is not in accordance with the Works Information or the applicable law – a part of the *works* designed by the *Contractor* which is not in accordance with the applicable law or the *Contractor*'s design which the *Project Manager* has accepted. ■ Defects are relevant to the period from Completion to the *defects date* because clause 43.2 states that Defects notified before Completion only need to be corrected **after** Completion (unless they would prevent the use of the *works*, in which case Completion cannot be achieved anyway). ■ Defects can be notified throughout the period from Completion to the *defects date*. ■ Section 4.10 details Defects notified before Completion. ■ Section 5.3 details Defects notified and/or corrected after Completion. ■ The *Supervisor*'s procedures when dealing with Defects after Completion are detailed in section 5.3.

Table 5.1 Continued

Defects Certificate	■ The *Supervisor* issues the Defects Certificate.
	■ It is issued to the *Contractor* and the *Project Manager*.
	■ It is issued on the *defects date* except where a Defect has been notified recently and the *defect correction period* for that Defect is not at an end at the *defects date*. In this case, the Defects Certificate is issued at the end of the *defect correction period*.
	■ The Defects Certificate contains a statement that there are no Defects; or where the *Contractor* has not corrected all Defects notified before the *defects date*, then the Defects Certificate lists those Defects.
	■ The *Employer*'s rights in respect of a Defect which the *Supervisor* has not found or notified (that is a latent defect) are not affected by the issue of the Defects Certificate.
	■ The Defects Certificate triggers the final payment to the *Contractor*.
defect correction period	■ Notified Defects must be corrected within the *defect correction period*.
	■ The use of italics in the term *defect correction period* indicates that the parties can find the relevant timescale in the Contract Data.
	■ Contract Data part one provides the *defect correction period*, which may appear as one period for all Defects (e.g. two weeks) or as a series of periods depending on the categorisation of the Defect.
	■ On discovery of a Defect, the *Contractor*'s obligations are set out in clause 43: – The *Contractor* is required to correct within the *defect correction period* all Defects which are notified by the *Supervisor*. – The *Contractor* is required to correct within the *defect correction period* all Defects which are notified by the *Contractor*. – The *Contractor* is required to correct all Defects even if they have not been notified, but the period for correction is not stated.
	■ For Defects notified before Completion, the *defect correction period* starts at Completion. For Defects notified after Completion, the *defect correction period* starts on notification, although access restrictions after Completion may prevent timeous correction.

5.2.   Defects before Completion

The notification and correction of Defects before Completion is discussed at section 4.10. There is some repetition in this section so that this section can stand on its own.

5.2.1   Summary

Any Defects notified and corrected before Completion affect the activities after Completion.

■ There may be some Defects that were notified before Completion which now have to be corrected.

■ Under clause 43.2 there is the potential that all Defects except those preventing use of the *works* will need to be corrected within the same time period after Completion. This could be very burdensome for the *Contractor* and the *Supervisor*.

■ The *Supervisor* and the *Project Manager* need to be aware that for Defects to be corrected after Completion, restricted access to correct the Defects may affect the time within which they can be corrected.

5.2.2   What happens at Completion

Completion marks the point between two categories of Defects (Figure 5.2). These are not contractual categories, although they could be if the *Employer* chose to include the distinction in the Works Information with the goal of

Figure 5.2 Correction of Defects notified after Completion

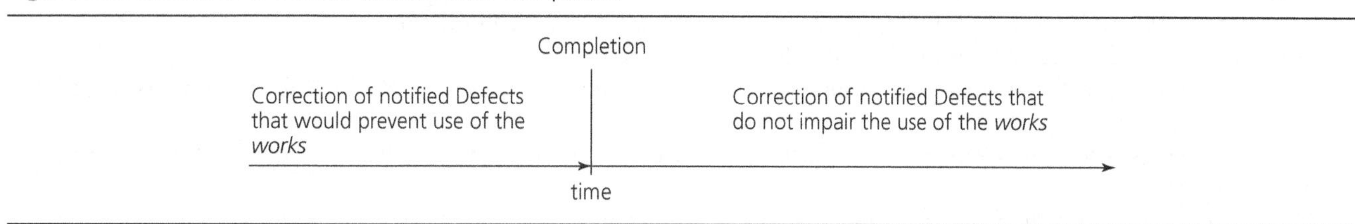

bringing more understanding to what the *Employer* considers to be Completion. Rather, Completion separates Defects that have already been notified which would prevent the *Employer* or Others from using the *works*, and Defects that have already been notified which can be corrected after Completion with no detriment to the project or the *works*.

5.2.3 Accounting for Defects corrected before Completion

The *defect correction period* only begins at Completion for Defects which were notified before Completion (clause 43.2). If the *Supervisor* feels strongly that a Defect notified before Completion should also be corrected before Completion, he has the following options.

- The *Supervisor* could include his preference for a pre-Completion correction on his Defect notification, but there is still no contractual requirement for it to be corrected before Completion.
- The *Supervisor* could issue a separate instruction requiring the Defect to be corrected prior to Completion, and the *Contractor* is required to obey the instruction if the instruction is deemed to be in accordance with the contract. (There is no requirement to copy the instruction to the *Project Manager*, therefore the *Project Manager* could be unaware that an instruction has been given.)
- The *Supervisor* could notify the Defect in the expectation that the *Project Manager* will only allow Completion to take place if the Defect is not severe enough to prevent use of the *works*.
- The *Supervisor* could instruct a search.

There is no other sanction on the *Contractor* if he does not correct a Defect before Completion.

The ECC allows the *Supervisor* to notify Defects, and it allows categorisation of Defects to facilitate a different *defect correction period*. The categorisation could be as simple as this:

Category A – 7 days
Category B – 3 weeks
Category C – 2 months.

The *Contractor* must correct Defects before the end of their *defect correction period*, but this period, however categorised, only begins at Completion for Defects notified before Completion.

5.3. Defects after Completion

Sections 5.1 and 5.2 discussed the role of the *Supervisor* in the *Project Manager*'s decision that Completion has been reached. This section discusses the role of the *Supervisor* after Completion in reaching the *defects date*.

5.3.1 Introduction

The *Supervisor* will receive a copy of the *Project Manager*'s certificate of Completion, which will provide the date of Completion. The *Supervisor* knows that all notified Defects that were not corrected before Completion will now have to be completed and their *defect correction period* started on the date of Completion written on the Completion certificate. Any further Defects notified will have to be corrected within their *defect correction period* and this period starts when the Defect is notified.

The *Supervisor* will also receive a copy of the *Project Manager*'s take over certificate. The certificate will certify the date of take over, which must take place no more than two weeks after the date of Completion. The *Supervisor* will thus understand the change in access rights for the *Contractor* for the purposes of correcting Defects.

The ECC allows for the following categories of Defects.

1. Defects notified before Completion which would prevent use of the *works* and which would therefore need to be corrected before Completion.
2. Defects notified before Completion which have been accepted and for which the Works Information has therefore been amended.
3. Defects notified before Completion which would not prevent the use of the *works* and which are not required to be corrected before Completion and must therefore be rectified after Completion.
4. Defects notified after Completion to be corrected after Completion.
5. Defects notified after Completion which have been accepted and for which the Works Information has therefore been amended.
6. Notified Defects where the *Contractor* has been given access to correct it but he has not corrected it within its *defect correction period*.
7. Notified Defects where the *Contractor* has not been given access to correct it.

Categories 1 and 2 were discussed in section 4.10. The following sections discuss categories 3 to 7.

5.3.2 Defects notified before Completion which must be corrected after Completion

Once Completion has been reached and certified by the *Project Manager*, the project team can carry out any remaining activities which did not prevent Completion, such as correcting Defects which were notified before Completion but which were not required to be corrected before Completion.

The ECC allows all Defects which do not prevent Completion being reached to be corrected after Completion.

If there is only one *defect correction period* stated in the Contract Data, then every Defect notified before Completion must be corrected during the same time period. It is possible that the list of Defects which need to be corrected after Completion could be daunting and, because the *defect correction period* for all of them starts at the same time, a lot of rework will be concentrated into a small time window. If there are different categories of Defects, with different *defect correction period*s, then correction may be less frantic, but still onerous.

Actions for the *Supervisor*	To-do list for the *Supervisor*
■ Continue to check the *works* and notify any Defects which have developed since Completion. ■ Ask the *Contractor* to share his programme of Defect correction so that the *Supervisor* can be in the right area of the Site to check off any Defect correction. ■ Perform any tests/inspections, notifying the *Contractor* beforehand as required and afterwards of the results.	■ Make sure that the list of notified Defects is up to date and in a format that can be checked as time goes by. ■ Make sure the list of Defects separately lists those which need to be corrected immediately after Completion and those which can wait a while so that the *Supervisor* can concentrate his time on the more urgent set of Defects. ■ Programme any tests/inspections still to be carried out.

5.3.3 Defects notified after Completion to be corrected after Completion

The notification of Defects is allowed until the *defects date*. Both the *Supervisor* and the *Contractor* can notify Defects. The *Contractor*'s obligation to correct Defects within the *defect correction period* is unchanged no matter who notified the Defect, and any Defects notified by either party must be corrected within the appropriate *defect correction period*.

The last day for notifying Defects is on the *defects date*. In this case, the Defects Certificate will be issued when the *defect correction period* for that Defect expires, rather than on the *defects date*.

During the period between Completion and the *defects date*, Defects can still be accepted, as described in clause 44, and there may also be access issues. In other words:

■ the *Contractor* can suggest to the *Project Manager* that he change the Works Information to accept a Defect
■ the *Project Manager* can suggest to the *Contractor* that the Works Information is changed to accept a Defect
■ if access is provided to the *Contractor* to correct a Defect and the *Contractor* does not correct it at all or correction is taking longer than the *defect correction period* then the *Employer* may hire in another contractor to complete the rectification
■ if access cannot be provided to the *Contractor* then the *Employer* may treat the Defect as being corrected.

Actions for the *Supervisor*	To-do list for the *Supervisor*
■ Agree with the *Project Manager* and the *Employer* his intended routine after Completion in terms of being on Site and continuing to look for Defects (and check off Defects which have been corrected by the *Contractor* post-Completion). ■ Attend the Site to check the *works*. ■ Notify Defects. ■ Receive Defect notifications from the *Contractor*. ■ Check off corrected Defects.	■ Prepare the list of Defects so that it can include Defects notified after Completion.

5.3.4 Notified Defects which have been accepted (clause 44.2)

The acceptance of Defects before Completion is addressed in section 4.10.

The process of accepting Defects is the same where Defects are to be corrected after Completion, whether they were notified before or after Completion.

1. The *Contractor* or the *Supervisor* notifies a Defect to the other.
2. The *Contractor* or the *Project Manager* proposes to the other that the Works Information is changed in order to accept the Defect.
3. If the *Project Manager* and the *Contractor* are prepared to consider the change, the *Contractor* submits a quotation for reduced Prices or an earlier Completion Date or both to the *Project Manager* for acceptance.
4. If the *Project Manager* accepts the quotation then he gives an instruction to change the Works Information, the Prices and the Completion Date accordingly.

What the Supervisor *does*
Although the *Supervisor* is not required to act under this clause, he should ask the *Project Manager* to be informed of and party to any discussions about accepting a Defect.

Table 5.2 describes an example process for accepting Defects which were notified after Completion. Note that not all actions are described in the ECC.

Table 5.2 An example process for accepting Defects

Process no.	Clause	*Supervisor*	*Contractor*	*Project Manager*	*Employer*
1	42.2	Notifies a Defect to the *Contractor*	Notifies a Defect to the *Supervisor*		
	Not part of ECC	The *Supervisor* communicates the Defect notification to the *Project Manager*			
	Not part of ECC	Notification to the *Employer* that the *Contractor* will need access to the *works* in order to correct the Defect			
2	33.1				Allows access
3	43.2		The *defect correction period* for the Defect starts on notification or, if take over has taken place, it starts when the necessary access and use have been provided		
4	44.1	Suggests to the *Project Manager* that the Works Information is changed in order to accept the Defect	Suggests to the *Contractor* that the Works Information is changed in order to accept the Defect		
	Not part of ECC	The *Supervisor* could make the same suggestion to both the *Project Manager* and the *Contractor*, who can then follow the process			
5	44.2		Prepared to consider the change	Prepared to consider the change	
6	44.2		Submits quotation to the *Project Manager* for change to Prices		
7a	44.2			Accepts and gives instruction to change the Works Information and Prices	
7b	44.2			Does not accept – no further action	

Table 5.2 Continued

Process no.	Clause	*Supervisor*	*Contractor*	*Project Manager*	*Employer*
Not part of ECC		At this point, depending on whether the actions take place just within each time period allowed (e.g. a *period for reply* of two weeks), the *defect correction period* may have expired. The *Contractor* must still correct the Defect and he may need access. Also, the *Supervisor* will need to be alerted that a Defect correction is still to take place. Therefore the following communications could take place.			
					Tells the *Supervisor* that the Defect has not been accepted
		Advises the *Contractor* that the *defect correction period* has restarted			
		Prompts the *Employer* to provide access	OR	Prompts the *Employer* to provide access	
	43.1		Corrects the Defect within its *defect correction period*		

- Ensure that accepting Defects is an agenda item for the regular meeting about Defects held with the *Project Manager*.
- Communicate with the *Contractor* so that he [the *Supervisor*] is aware of any accepted Defects where the appropriate communication with the *Project Manager* has not taken place.
- Suggest to the *Project Manager* that a Defect should be accepted, where this is appropriate.
- Keep track of any accepted Defects, especially where they impact on other parts of the *works*.

5.3.5 Notified Defects where the *Contractor* has been given access to correct it

This scenario is the same whether (1) the whole of the *works* has been taken over, (2) sectional Completion has taken place and a part of the *works* has been taken over, or (3) the *Employer* has taken over a part of the *works* through use (clause 35.2).

- The *Contractor* has been given access to correct a notified Defect but he has not corrected it within its *defect correction period*.
- The *Project Manager* assesses the cost to the *Employer* of having the Defect corrected by other people and the *Contractor* pays the amount. The Works Information is treated as having been changed to accept the Defect.

There are four scenarios in this table.

1. Where the *Contractor* is given delayed access.
2. Where the *Contractor* is given access and corrects the Defect.
3. Where the *Contractor* is given access and does not/cannot correct the Defect.
4. Where the *Contractor* is given access and does not/cannot correct the Defect within its *defect correction period*.

Table 5.3 Notified Defects where the *Contractor* has been given access to correct it

Process no.	Clause	*Supervisor*	*Contractor*	*Project Manager*	*Employer*
1	42.2	Notifies a Defect to the *Contractor*	Notifies a Defect to the *Supervisor*		
Not part of ECC		The *Supervisor* communicates the Defect notification to the *Project Manager*			
Not part of ECC		Notification to the *Employer* that the *Contractor* will need access to the *works* in order to correct the Defect			

Table 5.3 Continued

Process no.	Clause	Supervisor	Contractor	Project Manager	Employer
SCENARIO 1 (*Contractor* is given delayed access)					
2	43.4				Allows access, but there is a delay in providing the necessary access and use
3	43.2		The *defect correction period* for the Defect only starts on access so the time taken to correct the Defect cannot necessarily be forecast and this delay may affect other Defects or other contractors working on the asset		
4	43.1		Corrects the Defect within its *defect correction period*		
SCENARIO 2 (*Contractor* is given access and corrects the Defect)					
2	43.4				Allows access
3	43.2		The *defect correction period* for the Defect starts on access		
4	43.1		Corrects the Defect within its *defect correction period*		
SCENARIO 3 (*Contractor* is given access and does not/cannot correct the Defect)					
2	43.4				Allows access
3	43.2		The *defect correction period* for the Defect starts on access		
4	45.1		Defect not corrected		
5a			If the Defect cannot be corrected then the *Contractor* can propose that the Works Information is changed to accept the Defect	Other actions follow – see section 5.3.4.	
5b	45.1		Pays the amount	Assesses the cost of other people correcting the Defect	
6	45.1			Works Information treated as having been changed to accept the Defect	
SCENARIO 4 (*Contractor* is given access, does not/cannot correct within its *defect correction period*)					
2	33.1				Allows access
3	43.2		The *defect correction period* for the Defect starts on access		
4	45.1		The Defect is not corrected within its *defect correction period*		
Not part of ECC		The *Supervisor* and/or *Project Manager* notify the *Contractor* that the *defect correction period* can be extended if that will allow the Defect to be corrected			

Table 5.3 Continued

Process no.	Clause	*Supervisor*	*Contractor*	*Project Manager*	*Employer*
5a			If the Defect cannot be corrected then the *Contractor* can propose that the Works Information is changed to accept the Defect	Other actions follow – see section 5.3.4	
5b	45.1		Pays the amount	Assesses the cost of other people correcting the Defect	
6	45.1			Works Information treated as having been changed to accept the Defect	

Actions for the *Supervisor*

- Be aware of the area in which the Defect is located and keep track of whether it has been taken over and what access is available for the *Contractor* so that he [the *Supervisor*] can be proactive about working with the *Contractor* to correct Defects.
- Be aware of what Defects may need correcting by other and have an idea of what is required so that he [the *Supervisor*] can help the *Project Manager* in assessing the cost of correction by others, if so required.
- Maintain communications with the *Contractor* throughout the process.
- Do what is required by his personal contract, such as communication with the *Employer* about access, communication with the *Project Manager*.

5.3.6 Notified Defects where the *Contractor* has not been given access to correct it (clause 45.2)

If the *Contractor* has not been given access to correct a notified Defect before the *defects date*, the *Project Manager* assesses the cost to the *Contractor* of correcting the Defect and the *Contractor* pays this amount. The Works Information is treated as having been changed to accept the Defect.

Table 5.4 Notified Defects where the *Contractor* has not been given access to correct it

Process no.	Clause	*Supervisor*	*Contractor*	*Project Manager*	*Employer*
1	42.2	Notifies a Defect to the *Contractor*	Notifies a Defect to the *Supervisor*		
Not part of ECC		The *Supervisor* communicates the Defect notification to the *Project Manager*			
Not part of ECC		Notification to the *Employer* that the *Contractor* will need access to the *works* in order to correct the Defect			
2	43.2		The *defect correction period* for the Defect starts on access		
3	45.2		Does not correct the Defect		Does not allow access
4	45.2		Pays the amount	Assesses the cost of *Contractor* correcting the Defect	
5	45.2			Works Information treated as having been changed to accept the Defect	

Actions for the *Supervisor*

- Be aware of the areas in which Defects are located and whether access is possible so that he [the *Supervisor*] can be proactive about working with the *Contractor* to correct Defects.
- Be aware of what Defects may not be able to be corrected and assess how the Works Information can be altered to accommodate the Defects.
- Maintain communication with the *Contractor* throughout the process.
- Do what is required by his personal contract, such as communication with the *Employer* about access, communication with the *Project Manager*.

5.3.7 Alignment of personal and project contracts

Much of the process for correcting Defects after Completion will depend on how the *Employer* has chosen to set up his project team and the internal controls required. The Defect management process within the ECC is not always stream-lined between the *Project Manager* and the *Supervisor*, although it is always clear, thus meeting the clarity objective of the NEC3.

Although it is the *Supervisor* who notifies Defects and who should therefore have a presence on Site after Completion, it is the *Project Manager* who makes the decisions about accepting Defects and the *Employer* who makes decisions about access. The *Employer* needs to make sure that the personal contracts with the *Supervisor* and the *Project Manager* are drafted to interlock with the Works Information and the ECC so that Defects correction is addressed adequately and does not fall between contracts. Putting in place a communication strategy between the *Supervisor* and the *Project Manager* may be all that is required. See section 2.3.2 for more information on the interfacing of professional contracts.

5.4. Take over

Defects may affect take over, and take over may affect the correction of notified Defects. Although Completion must have been reached for take over to have taken place, the *Contractor* still has access to the *works* unless the Works Information provides otherwise. It is possible that once take over has taken place, access may be more limited, which may affect the performance and timing of the *Contractor* in correcting Defects.

5.4.1 Introduction to take over

What the contract says

- The *Employer* is required to take over the *works* not later than two weeks after Completion (clause 35.1).
- The *Employer* may choose to take over the *works* earlier than Completion. However, Contract Data part one may include a statement that the *Employer* is not willing to take over the *works* before the Completion Date if early take over is **not** acceptable (clause 35.1).
- The *Project Manager* certifies the date of take over within one week of the date of take over (clause 35.3).
- Since the *Project Manager* is required to copy all his certificates to the *Supervisor*, the *Supervisor* will be aware that take over has taken place (clause 13.6).
- In general, if the *Employer* starts to use the *works*, then he is deemed to have taken over that part of the *works* except for a reason stated in the Works Information (clause 35.2).

What the contract doesn't say

The ECC does not describe how take over is reached or any commissioning required, nor does it refer to any planned or reactive maintenance required in the period between Completion and the *defects date*.

Since take over is the responsibility of the *Project Manager*, the Works Information may describe actions for the *Contractor* and interactions between the *Contractor* and the *Project Manager*.

Examples of information that the *Contractor* may be requested to provide to the *Project Manager* are:

- take over documentation, such as that required by the CDM Regulations
- commissioning schedule
- as-installed drawings
- operating and maintenance manuals not already required for Completion
- warranties and guarantees.

Actions for the Supervisor

There are no actions for the *Supervisor* in relation to take over; however, take over affects future actions of the *Supervisor* and he needs to be aware when it takes place. The *Supervisor*'s personal contract may require actions of the *Supervisor* that are additional to those required by the ECC, such as to provide a list of outstanding Defects to the *Project Manager*. The Works Information may describe actions between the *Contractor* and the *Supervisor*.

5.4.2   How take over affects Defects management

After take over has taken place and the *Contractor* no longer has uncontrolled access to the Site, the Defect management process is just that little bit harder; for each Defect, the *Project Manager* has to arrange for the *Employer* to allow the *Contractor* access to and use of the part of the *works* where the Defect is located. Although the *defect correction period* is protected for the *Contractor* (as it begins when the necessary access and use have been provided), there may still be an impact on the *works*. Note that there should not be an impact on the *Employer*'s use of the *works* as Completion should not have been certified if there was a Defect that affected use of the *works*.

Sections 5.3.5 and 5.3.6 describe the *Supervisor*'s actions after take over with respect to Defects.

5.5.   The *defects date*

The *Supervisor* and the *Contractor* are required to notify Defects until the *defects date* and therefore this date marks the end of the *Supervisor*'s actions under the ECC.

5.5.1   Introduction to the *defects date*

What the contract says
- The *defects date* is the point specified in the contract up to which the *Contractor* and *Supervisor* will look for Defects and up to which they will notify Defects (clause 42.2).
- The *defects date* is identified in Contract Data part one under section 4. The *defects date* is stated number of weeks after Completion, e.g. 52 weeks.
- The *Supervisor* issues the Defects Certificate at the later of the *defects date* and the last *defect correction period*. The Defects Certificate is discussed in section 5.6 (clause 43.3).
- The *Employer*'s rights in terms of latent defects are protected (clause 43.3).

5.5.2   What is the *defects date*?

The *defects date* marks the end of the period after Completion within which the *Contractor* is liable for all Defects found in the *works* and notified by either the *Contractor* or the *Supervisor*. The *Contractor* still has an obligation to correct all Defects, whether they are notified or not. In other forms of contract this period is called the defects liability period.

The *defects date* is based on a period of time stated as weeks after Completion of the whole of the *works* and is therefore calculated from the date on which the *Project Manager* certifies that Completion has taken place; it is not calculated from the Completion Date (which would be the *completion date* included in the Contract Data amended as a result of any compensation events or acceleration).

If the *works* have been constructed with sectional completion, then the *defects date* is calculated from Completion of the whole of the *works*. Sections of the *works* which were completed earlier than the whole of the *works* are therefore subject to a longer period within which the *Contractor* is liable for Defects.

Actions for the *Supervisor*	To-do list for the *Supervisor*
- Mark the expected *defects date* on the wall calendar so that it is clearly visible. - Keep track of all Defects and check them off on the list of Defects. - In the month before the *defects date*, assess all Defects and when their *defect correction period* is due to end so that the *Supervisor* can compare this with the *defects date*.	- Be aware of the *defects date* in the Contract Data: defined as a number of weeks after Completion of the whole of the *works*. - Be aware of the date of Completion certified by the *Project Manager* in the Completion certificate, which would have been copied to the *Supervisor*, so that the approximate *defects date* can be calculated based on the *defects date* included in the Contract Data. - Make sure the list of Defects is up to date so that the last *defect correction period* is easily discernible.

5.6.   The Defects Certificate

It is the *Supervisor* who issues the Defects Certificate.

5.6.1 Introduction to the Defects Certificate

What the contract says

- The *Supervisor* issues the Defects Certificate at the later of the *defects date* and the end of the last *defect correction period* (clause 43.3).
- The Defects Certificate is either a list of Defects that the *Supervisor* has notified before the *defects date* and which the *Contractor* has not corrected or, if there are no such Defects, a statement that there are none (clause 11.2(6)).
- The *Supervisor* will issue the Defects Certificate to the *Contractor* and the *Project Manager* (clause 13.6).
- The *Project Manager* assesses the amount due [to the *Contractor*] four weeks after the *Supervisor* issues the Defects Certificate (clause 50.1).

5.6.2 When is the Defects Certificate issued and what does it comprise?

The *Supervisor* issues the Defects Certificate in accordance with these principles: if, at the date which is calculated to be the *defects date* (e.g. 52 weeks after Completion of the whole of the *works*):

Table 5.5 When the Defects Certificate can be issued and what it comprises

all notified Defects are corrected and there are no partly corrected Defects	then the Defects Certificate can be issued at the *defects date* and the certificate will include a statement that there are no Defects at that time
a notified Defect is not fully corrected and its *defect correction period* has not yet expired	then the Defects Certificate will not be issued at the *defects date*, but will be issued at the date that marks the end of that last *defect correction period* for the Defect notified on or before the *defects date*
a notified Defect is not fully corrected, its *defect correction period* has not yet expired and it is unlikely that it will be corrected within that time period	then the Defects Certificate will not be issued at that date, but will be issued at the date that marks the end of that *defect correction period* (whether or not that Defect is fully corrected by the end of that *defect correction period*) and the Defect will be included in the Defects Certificate as an uncorrected Defect. The *Project Manager*, in assessing the amount due four weeks after the Defects Certificate, has the right under clause 45.1 to assess the cost to the *Employer* of having any Defects listed on the Defects Certificate corrected by other people and to include that amount in his final payment certificate to be offset against any amount retained in accordance with secondary Option X16 (retention)

A sample Defects Certificate is included in Appendix 5E.

Figure 5.3 shows the interrelation of time and the correction of Defects leading to the Defects Certificate.

Figure 5.3 Timing of Completion and the *defects date* in relation to each Defect's *defect correction period*

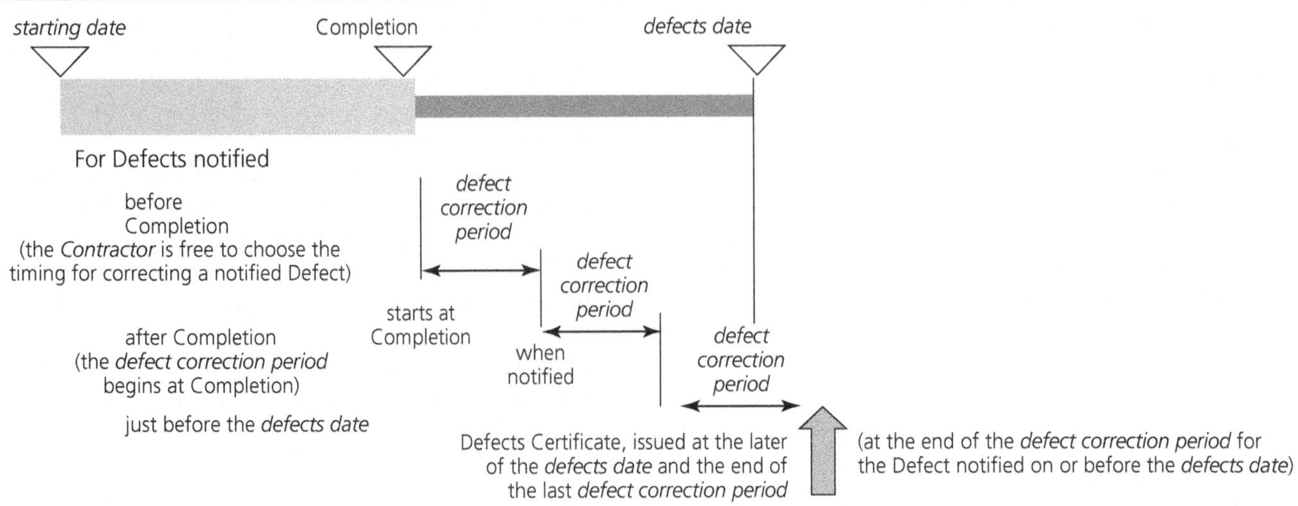

5.6.3   Implications of the issue of the Defect Certificate

The *Supervisor* should be aware of the following.

- The issue of the Defects Certificate does not relieve the *Contractor* of his responsibility under the contract to correct all Defects (clause 43.3).
- The *Employer*'s rights in respect of a Defect which the *Supervisor* has not found or notified are not affected by the issue of the Defects Certificate (clause 43.3).
- The Defects Certificate will be used by the *Project Manager* in assessing the final amount due to the *Contractor* (clause 50.1).

In carrying out his assessment of the amount due, the *Project Manager* will offset the cost of any uncorrected Defects against the release of the second half of the retention sufficient to cover the likely cost of uncorrected Defects at the *defects date*. Note that the cost of correcting Defects is the cost to the *Employer* of having the Defects corrected by other people and that this amount may be significantly different from the cost to the *Contractor* to correct the Defects himself.

The *Employer* may inform the *Contractor* of Defects after the *defects date* but the *Contractor*'s responsibility for them is limited by the operation of secondary Option X18 (Limitation of liability).

Total liability in this instance would include both the direct loss (always includes remedying the Defect) and the indirect or consequential losses which are not direct losses arising from a breach of contract.

5.6.4   Actions for the *Supervisor* and the *Project Manager*

Actions for the *Supervisor*	Actions for the *Project Manager*
<ul><li>Finalise the list of Defects so that any uncorrected Defects are clearly identifiable.</li><li>Identify any outstanding Defects and notify the *Contractor*.</li><li>Share outstanding Defects with the *Project Manager*, who can make an adjustment for the release of retention where costs have been or will be incurred by the *Employer* to have Defects corrected by someone other than the *Contractor*.</li><li>Consider any proposals from the *Contractor* for accepting Defects.</li><li>Arrange for the correction of Defects by other people.</li></ul>	<ul><li>Carry out an engineering review of the project, including:<ul><li>Has the *Contractor* fulfilled all his contractual obligations?</li><li>Is the project performing as expected?</li><li>Have any remedied Defects re-appeared, for example, beam cracking?</li></ul></li><li>Check that the following are all in place:<ul><li>insurances</li><li>collateral warranties</li><li>manufacturers' guarantees.</li></ul></li><li>Arrange for the return of the performance bond if required.</li></ul>

NEC3: The Role of the *Supervisor*
ISBN 978-0-7277-6096-8

Summary

It is commonly understood that the *Supervisor* is responsible for the quality of the *works*. In fact, it is the *Contractor* who is responsible for the quality of the *works*. Instead, the *Supervisor*'s role is to ensure – through the management of Defects and through the tests and inspections described in the contract – that the *works* are provided to the quality required by the Works Information and the applicable law.

The *Supervisor* is employed by the *Employer* and does not report to the *Project Manager*, but he must work alongside him. For the contract to work effectively, the *Supervisor* needs to undertake actions and communications that are not described in the contract. However, if the *Employer* expects these actions, then he must make sure that they are described in the *Supervisor*'s personal contract. Simply requiring the individual to undertake all of the actions required of the *Supervisor* in the ECC will not be enough.

Appendices

NEC3: The Role of the *Supervisor*
ISBN 978-0-7277-6096-8

ICE Publishing: All rights reserved
http://dx.doi.org/10.1680/nectrs.60968.093

Appendix 1
Supervisor actions in the ECC: clause details

ECC clause	*Supervisor* actions required
10.1 [The *Supervisor*] shall act as stated in the contract and in a spirit of mutual trust and co-operation.	As with all the other players in the contract – the *Contractor*, the *Project Manager* and the *Employer* – the *Supervisor* is required not only to do what the contract says he must do, but **also to behave in a co-operative, trustworthy and trusting way**. Arguably, the behaviour of the *Supervisor* has less impact on the outcome of the contract than the behaviour of the *Project Manager* and the *Contractor*; nevertheless, the *Supervisor*'s co-operation with the *Contractor* and the *Project Manager* can affect the success of the contract. In particular, many of the *Supervisor*'s interactions with the *Project Manager* are not specifically included in the ECC conditions and should be captured in the *Supervisor*'s personal contract with the *Employer*.
11.2 Definitions	Many of the definitions affect the *Supervisor*'s work under the contract, such as Completion, a Defect, the Defects Certificate and the Works Information, and any *Supervisor* should be very aware of the definitions and how they impact on the work of the *Supervisor*.
13.1 [The *Supervisor* is required] to communicate in a form which can be read, copied and recorded.	A form which can be read, copied and recorded means email (or other electronic means) or on paper (whether typed or handwritten). The *Supervisor* may wish to ascertain from the *Project Manager* what kind of communication systems are in place on the project and to whom communications should be copied.
13.3 [The *Supervisor* is required] to reply to a communication within the *period for reply*. 13.5 The *Project Manager* may extend the *period for reply* to a communication if the *Project Manager* and the *Contractor* agree to an extension before a reply is due. Note: the *Project Manager* will ascertain the facts from the *Supervisor* – hence the requirement for the *Supervisor* to keep good records of his actions.	The *Supervisor* is required to communicate with the *Contractor* on a number of issues (clauses 13.6, 14.2, 40.3, 42.1, 42.2, 43.3). Clause 13.3 provides that he must reply to communications within the period determined by the contract; and clause 13.5 provides for the *Project Manager* and the *Contractor* to agree an extension to the *period for reply*, but only if the extension takes place before the reply is due. Therefore, although the *Supervisor* is tied in to responding within a certain period, if he wants to extend that period through agreement with the *Contractor*, he has to ask the *Project Manager* to do it for him. A number of comments can be made at this point. ■ How will the *Project Manager* know that the *Contractor* is expecting a reply from the *Supervisor*? ■ How will the *Project Manager* know that he needs to agree to an extension of the *period for reply* with the *Contractor*? ■ What if the *Supervisor* and the *Contractor* agreed between them that the period in which the *Supervisor* is required to reply could be extended? ■ What if the *Contractor* notifies a compensation event to the *Project Manager* under clause 60.1(6) that states that if the communication does not take place within the required time parameters, this default may be a compensation event. However, the

ECC clause	*Supervisor* actions required
13.5 (*cont.*)	*Supervisor* is not involved in the procedure that follows the notification of a compensation event; and the *Project Manager* may not even know that the *Supervisor* has defaulted in his requirement to communicate timeously. It is very likely that the *Project Manager* will want to be aware of communications that affect the project and he may require the *Supervisor* to interact in a specific way on the project. The *Supervisor* also needs to be aware of other communication timescales in the Works Information.
13.6 [The *Supervisor* is required] to issue certificates to the *Project Manager* and the *Employer*.	There is no contractual mechanism for the *Supervisor* to communicate with the *Project Manager* about Defects, and tests and inspections and the only certificate required to be copied to the *Project Manager* is the Defects Certificate. This means that the *Project Manager* will not necessarily be aware of notified Defects and of tests and inspections being carried out. This emphasises the importance of project procedures and regular meetings, such as morning meetings or weekly meetings, where the *Project Manager* can be apprised of events or actions that will affect the progress of the *works* and the budget.
14.2 [The *Supervisor* is required] to notify the *Contractor* before delegating any actions or cancelling any delegation.	The *Project Manager* and the *Supervisor* can both delegate their actions and are required to let the *Contractor* know before they do this. The *Supervisor* on a large or complicated project may choose to delegate actions such as his marking of Plant and Materials outside the Working Areas (clause 71.1), especially if they are situated some distance from the Working Areas, perhaps even overseas.
14.4 [The *Employer* is required] to give notice to the *Contractor* before replacing the *Project Manager* or the *Supervisor*.	It is obviously important for the *Contractor* to know who the *Supervisor* is, to whom he has delegated actions (see clause 14.2) and who his replacement is, if the *Employer* chooses to replace the *Supervisor* at any point during the contract. Therefore the duty falls to the *Employer* to notify the *Contractor* that a replacement is going to take place.
16 Early warning	The early warning procedure described in clause 16 does not mention the *Supervisor* directly. There are actions for the *Contractor* and the *Project Manager* and they may instruct others (such as the *Supervisor*) to attend a risk reduction meeting. Early warnings are required for matters that will affect the cost and programme of the project and anything that may impair the performance of the *works* in use. The *Supervisor* is interested in all these things as they may require amendments to the Works Information and may therefore affect his checking for compliance with the Works Information. In any case, he should be able to: ■ contribute to discussions about avoiding or reducing 'the effect of the registered risks' on the Risk Register, and ■ make decisions on the actions to be taken and who will take them (some actions may inevitably fall to the *Supervisor*), and ■ generally help arrive at solutions that protect the *Employer*'s interests as represented by the Works Information. It may be sensible for the *Project Manager* to set up regular risk reduction meetings and ensure that he notifies the *Supervisor* of all risk reduction meetings and requests the *Supervisor*'s attendance where relevant as part of the administering of the project.

ECC clause	*Supervisor* actions required
17 Ambiguities and inconsistencies; 18 Illegal and impossible requirements	These clauses do not mention the *Supervisor* specifically and actions are required from the *Contractor* and the *Project Manager*. But the *Supervisor* may be able to contribute to discussions about: ■ ambiguities and inconsistencies in or between the Works Information, Site Information, Contract Data and any other documents that form part of the contract ■ decisions about whether the Works Information requires the *Contractor* to do anything that is illegal or impossible. As with clause 16, the *Project Manager* may choose to ask the *Supervisor* to attend any discussions as a matter of course, but this is not a contractual requirement and should therefore form part of the contract between the *Supervisor* and the *Employer*.
20 and 21 Design issues	The *Contractor* is required to Provide the Works in accordance with the Works Information (clause 20.1.), and to design the part of the *works* that the Works Information states he is to design (clause 21.1). These clauses dictate the *Contractor*'s fundamental duties and, indirectly, the *Supervisor*'s duties, as he will check that the *Contractor* has met these requirements. Clause 21.2 requires the *Project Manager* to accept the *Contractor*'s design (as long as the Works Information requires the *Contractor* to submit his design to the *Project Manager*). One of the reasons that the *Project Manager* may cite for not accepting the design is that it does not comply with the Works Information. Once again, the *Supervisor* may be involved in decisions about the design and the Works Information. In fact, the *Project Manager* may involve other professionals in his decisions about the design – designers, architects, engineers and specialists, such as fire or acoustics engineers. And, once again, the *Supervisor*'s involvement may be part of the contract between the *Supervisor* and the *Employer*.
27.2 [The *Contractor* is required] to provide access to the *works* to the *Project Manager*, *Supervisor* and Others.	The *Contractor* is required to provide access for the *Supervisor* to work being done and Plant and Materials being stored for the contract. Although this action is on the *Contractor*, the *Supervisor* may wish to communicate with the *Contractor* about access and perhaps give him indications of timings etc., especially for secure storage, which may be locked or otherwise secured.
27.3 [The *Contractor* is required] to obey instructions given by the *Project Manager* or the *Supervisor* which are in accordance with the contract.	This clause places an onus on the *Contractor* to obey instructions given by the *Supervisor*, in the knowledge that instructions must be in writing (or 'read, copied and recorded' as per clause 13.1). But note that there is no contractual requirement for the *Supervisor* to copy this instruction to the *Project Manager* (as clause 13.6 refers only to certificates). As with other communications already mentioned, it is likely that the *Project Manager* and the *Supervisor* will set up regular meetings or other methods of communication to keep each other apprised of their actions under the contract that may affect the project. There is only one clause that allows the *Supervisor* to give an instruction to the *Contractor* – clause 42.1.
30.2 Completion	It is the *Project Manager* who decides the date of Completion. But, given the definition of Completion, it is unlikely that he would want to do this in isolation. The *Supervisor* can undoubtedly contribute his opinion of whether: ■ the *Contractor* has 'done all the work which the Works Information states he is to do' and has ■ 'corrected notified Defects'.

ECC clause	*Supervisor* actions required
30.2 (*cont.*)	The list of Defects should not be very long, as it is likely that the *Contractor* will correct Defects as he goes along, and because the *Contractor* should correct Defects even if the *Supervisor* does not notify him of them. The Works Information should include what requirements have to be met to reach Completion; those requirements may be the extent of the Defects 'allowed' to reach Completion other than the ones that will prevent use of the *works*.
31.2 The programme	The programme includes information and dates of which the *Supervisor* may wish to take note in carrying out his duties. Examples include: the order and timing of operations; a statement on how the *Contractor* plans to do the work; and when tests and inspections will need to take place to progress the *works*. The *Supervisor* will need to understand the programme so that he knows when he needs to carry out his actions without delaying the *works*.
40 Tests and inspections	The procedure for tests and inspections described in core clause 40 only applies to those required by the Works Information or the applicable law. The *Supervisor* should make sure that the tests and inspections included in the Works Information will yield sufficient information about the quality of the *works*. If the Works Information and the applicable law, in the opinion of the *Supervisor*, will not provide enough information to determine the quality of the *works* (as required by the Works Information) then the *Supervisor* may wish to advise the *Employer* and *Project Manager* so that changes to the Works Information can be made.
40.2 The *Contractor* and the *Employer* provide materials, facilities and samples for the tests and inspections as stated in the Works Information.	The *Employer* is required to provide materials, facilities and samples for tests and inspections as stated in the Works Information, but there is no ECC contractual obligation on the *Supervisor* or the *Project Manager* to tell the *Employer* that the tests/inspections are imminent and he should get ready the things that the Works Information said would be provided by the *Employer*. This sort of communication should be agreed internally. Clause 60.1(16) allows a compensation event if materials, facilities and samples for tests and inspections required by the Works Information are not provided by the *Employer*. Clause 60.1(3) allows a compensation event if the *Employer* does not provide something that he is to provide by the date for providing it shown on the Accepted Programme. It seems likely that the *Project Manager*, in his role managing the programme, will give the *Employer* some notice to provide things required; it may even be part of the *Project Manager*'s duties under his contract with the *Employer* that it is the *Project Manager* who is responsible for ensuring that the appropriate things are provided. Otherwise, the *Supervisor* may need to inform the *Project Manager* that tests are imminent; this notification should be agreed between the *Supervisor* and the *Project Manager* prior to the start of the contract and should take place at a time that allows the things required to be provided in good time so as not to delay the test or inspection. The *Supervisor* and the *Project Manager* should both bear in mind that the tests and inspections can be repeated if a Defect is found (clause 40.4) and therefore the *Employer* may need to provide materials, facilities and samples a second time. The *Supervisor* should keep records and advise the *Project Manager* so that he can assess and deduct from payments the costs incurred by the *Employer* of such retests, etc.

ECC clause	*Supervisor* actions required
40.3 [The *Contractor* is required] to notify the *Supervisor* of tests and inspections before they start. [The *Contractor* is required] to notify the *Supervisor* of the results of tests and inspections. [The *Contractor* is required] to notify the *Supervisor* before doing work which would obstruct tests or inspections.	This is one of the clauses where notifications take place only between the *Contractor* and the *Supervisor*, without any contractual requirement to keep the *Project Manager* in the loop. For smaller projects, the *Project Manager* and the *Supervisor* may be the same person. On larger projects, the *Supervisor* and the *Project Manager* may want to agree some sort of routine about the tests and inspections so that the *Project Manager* is kept aware of what tests and inspections are taking place and their results. The *Supervisor* can carry out his own tests (described in the Works Information) even if the *Contractor* has done the same test as part of his own QMS.
40.3 [The *Supervisor* is required] to notify the *Contractor* of his tests and inspections before they start and afterwards of the results.	Even if the *Supervisor* were not required to provide the *Contractor* with notifications about tests and inspections, it would be a courtesy to do so, so that the *Contractor* can make preparations if required or be present to watch a test. The *Supervisor* is not contractually obliged to copy his notifications to the *Project Manager*, but the *Supervisor* and the *Project Manager* may agree a regular means of communication so that the *Project Manager* is kept in the loop. There is nothing stopping the *Contractor* watching the *Supervisor*'s tests. Indeed, where the *Supervisor*'s tests and inspections are required for payment to be made, the *Contractor* will wish to attend the *Supervisor*'s tests and inspections. The *Supervisor* may only carry out tests and inspections required by the Works Information or the applicable law; this stresses the importance of the Works Information to the *Supervisor*. The *Supervisor* may need to repeat a test or inspection if a Defect is found. Of course, if the *Contractor* and the *Project Manager* agree to accept the Defect, there is no need to repeat the test or inspection and the *Project Manager* will need to inform the *Supervisor* of his decision.
40.3 The *Supervisor* may watch any test done by the *Contractor*.	The wording of this clause means that: ■ the *Supervisor* may watch any test done by the *Contractor* as long as the test is required by the Works Information and the applicable law ■ if the *Contractor* chooses to carry out his own tests, which are not part of the Works Information or the applicable law, then the *Supervisor* has no contractual right to watch the test or inspection (but, in the spirit of mutual trust and co-operation, the *Contractor* may allow the *Supervisor* to watch in any case). There is no mention of inspections, but this does not mean that the *Supervisor* cannot watch inspections being carried out if the *Contractor* allows him to, and he will be notified of the results if the inspection was required by the Works Information or the applicable law. There is no mention of the *Contractor*'s right to watch tests or inspections carried out by the *Supervisor*, although he will be notified that they are going to take place and afterwards he will be notified of the results. However, in the spirit of mutual trust and co-operation, there is no reason why the *Supervisor* would stop the *Contractor* from observing.
40.4 Any test or inspection that shows a Defect is repeated after the Defect is corrected.	This clause is so simple, but there are so many things that must come together for the clause to work and achieve its intended result. The initial test or inspection: ■ can be one carried out by either the *Supervisor* or the *Contractor* and ■ must be one that is required by the Works Information and the applicable law.

ECC clause	*Supervisor* actions required
40.4 (*cont.*)	Let's say it is a test carried out by the *Supervisor*. If the *Employer* is to provide things for the test then the *Supervisor* will have notified the *Employer* and the *Project Manager* as relevant. The test shows that there is a Defect, for example, a part of the *works* that is not in accordance with the Works Information. ■ The *Supervisor* will notify the *Contractor* of the results of the test and inspections, that is that the test showed that a Defect exists. ■ The *Supervisor* should also notify the *Contractor* of the Defect (clause 42.2) because each contractual notification should be separately notified (clause 13.7). ■ Although not required by this clause 40.4, in order for other clauses to work, such as clause 40.6 and 40.2 and to avoid 60.1(16), the *Supervisor* should notify the *Project Manager* (a) that a required test has failed, (b) that the *Contractor* has been notified of the Defect, (c) that the test will have to be repeated and (d) that the *Employer* will have to provide things for the test repetition or will incur a cost for the test or inspection repetition. ■ The *Contractor* corrects the notified Defect within the *defect correction period*. This period is a stated period of time, for example two weeks, or there may be different periods for specified categories of Defects, as stated in Contract Data part one. ■ Contractually, the *defect correction period* for Defects notified before Completion only starts at Completion. However, the *Contractor* has other obligations, such as meeting Conditions by the Key Date and making sure that Completion is on or before the Completion Date and it may be more efficient to correct the Defect and carry out the retest immediately. ■ The *Supervisor* should be aware of the Defect correction so that he can notify the *Contractor* that he is going to carry out the retest. Even though the retest or reinspection was not due to actions of the *Supervisor*, the *Supervisor* still has to carry out the test or inspection without causing unnecessary delay to the *works* (clause 40.5) and he may have to juggle conflicting priorities. ■ In addition, where the *Employer* incurs a cost because of the repeated test or inspection, then the *Project Manager* assesses the cost of the repeated test or inspection and it is paid by the *Contractor* (see clause 40.6). As part of the process, the *Supervisor* should then ensure that the *Employer* and the *Project Manager* are suitably and timeously notified so that the provision by the *Employer* of things required for the test does not delay the *works* further. ■ The testing and inspection procedure starts again and the retest/reinspection is carried out by the *Supervisor*, who then notifies the result to the *Contractor*. Assuming the retest or reinspection does not show a Defect, the *Contractor* carries on with the *works*.
40.5 To do tests and inspections without causing unnecessary delay to work or payment.	The *Supervisor* must ensure that the tests and inspections which he is required to carry out in accordance with the applicable law or the Works Information take place without 'unnecessary delay' to the work being done and also to a payment which is conditional upon a test or inspection being successful. Of course, it may be difficult to determine what would be agreed to be a 'necessary' delay so that a clause 60.1(11) compensation event does not arise. For the *Contractor* to evidence that the *Supervisor* has not carried out his test/inspection timeously, the *Contractor* may have to use the Accepted Programme, the *Supervisor*'s notification of the test/inspection and the date of the actual test/inspection. The *Supervisor* should keep the *Project Manager* informed of all his actions. Clause 40.5 also refers to the situation of a *Supervisor* not carrying out the test/inspection at all, but only where payment to the *Contractor* is conditional upon the test/inspection being successful: where the test/inspection has not been done by the *Supervisor* and the delay is not the *Contractor*'s fault, the payment becomes due at

ECC clause	*Supervisor* actions required
40.5 (*cont.*)	the later of the *defects date* and the end of the last *defect correction period*. This may seem unduly harsh, but when viewed against the backdrop of a clause 60.1(11) compensation event, it can be recognised that it is only at the end of the *defects date* or the end of the last *defect correction period* that the *Project Manager* can be sure that the work has passed the test/inspection that was not done by the *Supervisor*.
40.6 [The *Project Manager* is required] to assess the cost incurred by the *Employer* in repeating a test or inspection after a Defect is found.	The ECC requires that the *Project Manager* must assess the cost incurred by the *Employer* in repeating a test/inspection after a Defect is found and that the *Contractor* must pay the amount. However, the contract does not dictate the whole process, and there are several things that need to come together for the *Project Manager* to be able to assess the cost of the repeated test. For this to take place, and unless the Works Information requires differently (such as imposing a requirement that the *Project Manager* and the *Employer* are notified about tests), the following needs to happen. ■ The taking place of the test or inspection must incur a cost to the *Employer*. ■ The *Supervisor* must notify the *Project Manager* (and perhaps the *Employer*) that the *Contractor* has failed a test or inspection, needs to correct the Defect and will need to retake the test or inspection, thus incurring a cost to the *Employer*. ■ The cost incurred by the *Employer* should be easily discernible from records of costs or must be included in either the Works Information or the *activity schedule/bill of quantities* as an assumption of cost accepted by the *Contractor*. ■ The *Supervisor* should keep records of cost involved in repeating a test or inspection. ■ The *Project Manager* (or perhaps a quantity surveyor/cost consultant if the *Project Manager* has delegated this duty along with the duties relating to core clause section 5) will assess the cost to the *Employer* of the repeated test or inspection, whether the cost arises from the provision of things such as consumables or the use of facilities, services, materials, utilities, fuel, etc. ■ The *Project Manager* will need to ensure that the cost assessed is included in his payment certificate, whether or not it has been included in the *Contractor*'s application for payment, so that the last part of clause 40.6 can be fulfilled and the *Contractor* pays the cost assessed as being the cost of the repeated test or inspection.
41.1 [The *Contractor* is required] to wait for notification from the *Supervisor* before bringing to the Working Areas those Plant and Materials that the Works Information states are to be inspected or tested before delivery. 41.1 [The *Supervisor* is required] to notify the *Contractor* of the results of the test or inspection on Plant and Materials required by the Works Information to be tested or inspected before delivery.	This clause is dependent on the following. ■ The Works Information must state that there are Plant and Materials that need to be tested/inspected before they can be delivered to the Working Areas. ■ Note that the clause does not confine the test/inspection to those to be carried out by the *Supervisor*; nor does it confine the test/inspection to tests/inspections required by the Works Information or the applicable law, as required by core clause 40. In addition, there is no requirement for the *Supervisor* to be present to watch the test/inspection. But the Works Information may impose all those obligations. ■ The Plant and Materials must pass the test/inspection. ■ The *Supervisor* must become aware that the test/inspection has been passed. This can take place in a number of ways, including simply that a certificate issued by an official body is available and pertinent to the described Plant and/or Materials. ■ The *Supervisor* must notify the *Contractor* that the test/inspection has been passed for those Plant/Materials. ■ The *Contractor* can then bring to the Working Areas those Plant and Materials. There are other actions that may help the *Project Manager* manage the project as well as he can. It is recommended that the *Supervisor* tells the *Project Manager* (e.g. through including him in the notification to the *Contractor* that the test/inspection was passed) that the Plant/Materials have passed the test, and therefore the *Project Manager* can expect the Plant/Materials to be delivered to the Working Areas. Late

ECC clause	*Supervisor* actions required
41.1 *(cont.)*	notification by the *Supervisor* can cause delay; however, the *Contractor*, in a spirit of mutual trust and co-operation, may choose to advise the *Supervisor* or the *Project Manager* that delay is imminent. In addition, if the test/inspection is one of those falling within the description of clause 40 (that is required by the Works Information or the applicable law), then the more stringent procedures required by that clause will also need to be followed.
42.1 [The *Contractor* is required] to carry out searches as instructed by the *Supervisor*. 42.1 [The *Supervisor*] may instruct the *Contractor* to search for a Defect and is required to give reasons for instructed searches.	Clause 42.1 allows the *Supervisor* to instruct the *Contractor* to search for a Defect, and the clause describes what 'searching' means and that things may need to be provided to carry out the test. The clause requires the *Supervisor* to provide reasons for his instruction, but it does not restrict the type of reasons. Clause 60.1(10) provides that an instructed search that does not yield a Defect is a compensation event unless the search is required only because the *Contractor* did not give sufficient notice that he was going to do work that would cover a required test/inspection. The clause may be applied as follows. - The *Contractor* has not given insufficient notice of doing work that will obstruct the *Supervisor* carrying out a test/inspection, but the *Supervisor* thinks something is wrong and issues an instruction to the *Contractor* to search for a Defect, stating his reasons on the instruction. - The *Supervisor* is not contractually required to alert the *Project Manager* to his concerns; however, it would be sensible if the *Supervisor* were to copy his instruction to the *Project Manager*. Whether or not a Defect is found, the additional activity and time taken to search and/or correct a Defect could affect the Accepted Programme and the *Project Manager* needs to understand the implications of the *Supervisor*'s actions. - In addition, the *Employer* is required to provide facilities for the search to take place and the *Supervisor* should advise the *Employer* and the *Project Manager* of the search and the required facilities so that the instructed search does not delay the programme any more than necessary. - The *Contractor* undertakes the search for a Defect and finds a Defect. Under clause 42.2, the *Contractor* notifies the *Supervisor* immediately. Under clause 43.2, the *Contractor* is free to correct the Defect at any time before Completion to suit his on-site activities; however, due to the nature of the work (that is that the Defect can be covered by other work), it makes more sense to correct the Defect immediately so that the work can progress. - Where the searching for and correction of a Defect involves a test/inspection and/or the provision of facilities by the *Employer* and these fall within the parameters of clause 40, the *Project Manager* may assess costs as provided for within clause 40.6. - A fully apprised *Project Manager* may ask the *Contractor* to provide some indication of how he intends to get back on track with the Accepted Programme, considering the time lost in the search and subsequent correction of the Defect.
42.2 Until the *defects date*, the *Contractor* is required to notify the *Supervisor* of Defects he finds as soon as he finds them. 42.2 Until the *defects date*, the *Supervisor* is required to notify the *Contractor* of Defects he finds as soon as he finds them.	Both the *Contractor* and the *Supervisor* are obliged to notify the other of a Defect 'as soon as he finds it'. As simple as these notifications are, the ramifications can be complex and time-consuming: the *Contractor* is required to correct a Defect whether or not the *Supervisor* notifies him of the Defect (clause 43.1); under clause 43.2 the *Contractor* is free to choose the timing of correcting a notified Defect up to Completion. After Completion the *Contractor* has to correct notified Defects outstanding at Completion within the *defect correction period* (although Completion cannot be achieved if any 'notified Defects' will prevent the *Employer* from using the *works* and prevent Others from doing their work (clause 11.2(2)). The notification of Defects is required to be communicated and notified separately from other communications.

ECC clause	*Supervisor* actions required

42.2 (*cont.*)	Therefore, although the *Supervisor* must ensure that work done tallies with the Works Information, he cannot necessarily enforce Defect correction. All he can do is provide the *Contractor* with notification that he [the *Supervisor*] has found a Defect; or instruct the *Contractor* to search for a Defect if he suspects that a Defect (now covered) has not been corrected.
	
	The *Contractor* decides when to correct the notified Defects (this is very sensible as the *Contractor* is in the best position to decide when to correct a notified Defect so as not to disrupt the *works*), as long as he corrects:
	
	■ Defects that were not notified by the *Supervisor* (e.g. Defects that the *Supervisor* missed but the *Contractor* has noticed) or Defects that the *Contractor* noticed before the *Supervisor* has checked that area of the *works* and
	■ all 'notified' Defects before the end of the *defect correction period*, bearing in mind that this only need start at Completion (for Defects notified before Completion), which means that:
	  – this applies only to 'notified' Defects (notified by either the *Contractor* or the *Supervisor*) but not those missed by the *Supervisor* and not admitted to by the *Contractor* through notification
	  – the *Supervisor* cannot enforce correction before this time (without a compensation event and the attendant time and cost implications), even if he thinks that the fault will prevent the *Contractor* from reaching Completion (e.g. the *Employer* will be prevented from using the *works* if a notified Defect is not corrected)
	  – unless there is thorough communication between the *Supervisor* and the *Project Manager* with regards to Defects and the alliance of the *works* with the Works Information, the *Project Manager* may not have a very good understanding of the progression of the *works*.
	
	It may also be worth the *Supervisor* and the *Contractor* agreeing to a regular meeting where Defects can be notified and discussed so that a joint way forward can be agreed upon. The *Supervisor* will find his job easier if the *Project Manager* also attends the meeting as the *Supervisor* will be able to keep him apprised of the status and progress of the *works* from his point of view.

43.1 [The *Contractor* is required] to correct Defects. 43.2 [The *Contractor* is required] to correct notified Defects before the end of the *defect correction period*.	Clause 43.1 obliges the *Contractor* to correct all Defects, whether notified by the *Contractor*, notified by the *Supervisor* or not notified at all. It is the next clause, 43.2, which imposes a timescale, both in terms of the amount of time that the *Contractor* is allowed to correct the Defect and when in the Accepted Programme the correction must take place. The *defect correction period* is stated in Contract Data part one and is therefore decided by the *Employer* in accordance with the length and complexity of the project. If Defects have been banded or categorised and a different *defect correction period* applies depending on the scale/type/area or criticality of the Defect, then the *Supervisor* will want to be specific in his Defect notification so that neither the *Contractor* nor the *Supervisor* can be in doubt about the length of time within which a *Contractor* must correct the Defect. This is not to say that the *Supervisor* may not provide some leniency or practicality in his Defect notification. For example, if the *Supervisor* sees a cosmetic or otherwise non-fatal Defect in a part of the Site where the *Contractor* is not currently working but is scheduled to work in a fortnight, then the *Supervisor* may, in his Defect notification, allow the *Contractor* to correct the Defect before the *Contractor* leaves that second part of the Site even where Contract Data part one, in accordance with the categorisation of the Defect, requires correction sooner.

ECC clause	*Supervisor* actions required
43.2 (*cont.*)	Clause 43.2 requires the *Contractor* to correct all Defects that were notified before Completion at Completion. Alternatively, the correction of Defects notified after Completion commences at the time when the Defect notification is made. Depending on the type of project, its length and complexity, the *Supervisor* may prefer that Defects are corrected through the course of the project rather than only at Completion, but this cannot be enforced unless the *Supervisor* can demonstrate that work would cover the Defect, thus not allowing work to continue before correction, or that Completion would not be achieved within the Accepted Programme if the Defect is not corrected before the *Contractor* progresses the *works*. Where the *Supervisor* is involved in the setting up of the project, this may be one of the areas where he may wish to ensure that he has good options when it comes to Defect correction.
43.3 [The *Supervisor* is required] to issue the Defects Certificate at the later of the *defects date* and the last *defect correction period*.	Clause 43.3 simply provides the *Supervisor* with the option of (a) closing the project at the end of the period of time foreseen by Contract Data part one, for example, 52 weeks after Completion, or (b) waiting until the *defect correction period* of the last applicable Defect notified has passed. Given the period of time between Completion and the *defects date*, it is hoped that the *Supervisor* is satisfied that the project has met the requirements of the Works Information and is content to sign it off by issue of the Defects Certificate, with the knowledge that his actions affect payment to the *Contractor*. The *Contractor* is entitled to receive the second half of the retention monies at the date of the Defects Certificate if secondary Option X16 applies to the project. The *Project Manager* will know that the Defects Certificate has been issued as the *Supervisor* is required to copy his certificates to the *Project Manager* (clause 13.6). The *Project Manager* is involved one last time in the project, to assess the amount due four weeks after the *Supervisor* issues the Defects Certificate (clause 50.1).
43.4 [The *Project Manager* is required] to arrange for the *Employer* to allow access and use to the *Contractor* of any part of the *works* needed for the correction of Defects after taking over.	This obligation of the *Project Manager* only affects the *Supervisor* because the *defect correction period* begins only when the necessary access and use have been provided. Whether the *Employer* takes over the *works* before the Completion Date or within two weeks after the Completion Date, the *Supervisor* needs to be aware that a Defect notified by the *Contractor* or the *Supervisor* after take over could take longer to correct simply because the *Employer* might not be able to provide access immediately to the *Contractor* to correct the Defect.
44.1 [The *Contractor*] may propose to the *Project Manager* that Works Information should be changed to avoid correction of a Defect. 44.1 [The *Project Manager*] may propose to the *Contractor* that Works Information should be changed to avoid correction of a Defect.	Clause 44 describes the procedure that takes place for accepting a Defect. The contractual actions are for the *Contractor* and the *Project Manager* and there are no contractual actions for the *Supervisor*, even though it is likely that it was the *Supervisor* who notified the Defect in the first place and that it will be the *Supervisor* who will check any further work done by the *Contractor* to accept the Defect. A good *Project Manager* will involve the *Supervisor* in any discussions about accepting Defects, and it is possible that the idea to accept a Defect may originate with the *Supervisor*, whether on Site with the *Contractor* or in regular discussions with the *Project Manager*. In any case, there is no doubt that the *Supervisor* will contribute positively to the described procedure to accept a Defect. The *Project Manager* should advise the *Supervisor* of the change in the Works Information so that the *Supervisor* can monitor the work done with reference to the

ECC clause	*Supervisor* actions required
44.2 [The *Contractor* is required] to submit a quotation for reduced Prices or an earlier Completion Date or both. 44.2 [The *Project Manager* is required] to give an instruction to change the Works Information, the Prices and the Completion Date if a quotation for not correcting Defects is accepted.	Works Information. The *Supervisor* should also be made aware of any change to the Completion Date (and therefore, potentially, Completion) since clause 43.2 requires the *defect correction period* of Defects notified before Completion to begin at Completion.
45.1 [The *Project Manager* is required] to assess the cost of having Defects corrected by other people if the *Contractor* fails to correct notified Defects within the *defect correction period* even though access was given. 45.1 [The *Contractor* is required] to pay the assessed costs of notified Defects being corrected by other people because they were not corrected within the *defect correction period* even though access was given. 45.2 [The *Project Manager* is required] to assess the cost of correcting a Defect where the *Contractor* was not given access to correct it. 45.2 [The *Contractor* is required] to pay the cost assessed of correcting a Defect where access was not given.	Clause 45 describes two scenarios, where the consequences are: (a) the *Project Manager* assesses the cost of correcting the Defect; (b) the *Contractor* pays the amount; and (c) the Works Information is treated as having been changed to accept the Defect. The two scenarios are: ■ Described in clause 45.1 (on the assumption that Completion and take over have taken place but the Defects Certificate has not been issued and a Defect is notified to the *Contractor*) – the *Contractor* has been given access to correct the Defect but does not correct the Defect within its *defect correction period*. It is likely that the response of the *Project Manager* and the *Supervisor* will depend on the circumstances. For example, the *Contractor* (a) simply does not attempt to correct the Defect, (b) begins to correct the Defect but cannot complete the correction within the *defect correction period*, or (c) begins to correct the Defect but cannot complete the correction at all, even if given more time. Even though the *Supervisor* is not contractually involved in clause 45, it is likely that the *Project Manager* will liaise with the *Supervisor* to deal with the intricacies of the scenario and the Defect correction. ■ Described in clause 45.2 (on the same assumptions) – the *Employer* is unable to give the *Contractor* access to correct a Defect (with no restrictions on reasons). The *Supervisor*'s contributions may not be quite as involved in this scenario, but the *Project Manager* may wish to take advice from the *Supervisor* regarding how the Defect could be corrected in order that he (the *Project Manager*) can assess accurately the cost of correcting the Defect.
50.1 The *Project Manager*'s assessment of the amount due	There are very few clauses in section 5 of the core clauses that require input from the *Supervisor* and, indeed, he is not mentioned at all in the section 5 clauses. However, the *Supervisor* may have a role to play, depending on how the *Project Manager* prefers to manage the project. For example, for Option A, the *Project Manager* is required to assess the amount due based on activities that are complete, that is which are without Defects that would (a) delay immediately following work or (b) be covered by immediately following work; the assessment for Option B is similar. Options C, D and E all involve Disallowed Costs for the correction of Defects after Completion; and, of course, a popular amendment disallows any Defect correction. For any of these Options, the *Project Manager* may wish to seek the *Supervisor*'s counsel regarding the presence of Defects or the correction of Defects.

ECC clause	*Supervisor* actions required
60 Compensation events	A number of compensation events can originate from actions or non-actions of the *Supervisor*. These are listed here and are discussed at section 4.7. 60.1(1) Accept Defect (strictly the *Project Manager*, but it is likely that the *Supervisor* will have significant input; and an instruction given by the *Project Manager* to accept a Defect is not a compensation event). 60.1(3) Provide something (strictly the *Employer*, but the *Supervisor* may have input where the things to be provided are for testing, searching or other actions of the *Supervisor*). 60.1(6) The *Supervisor* does not reply to a communication from the *Contractor* within the period required by the contract. 60.1(8) The *Supervisor* changes a decision that he has previously communicated to the *Contractor*. 60.1(10) The *Supervisor* instructs the *Contractor* to search for a Defect and no Defect is found (unless the search is needed only because the *Contractor* gave insufficient notice of doing work obstructing a required test or inspection). 60.1(11) A test or inspection done by the *Supervisor* causes unnecessary delay. 60.1(12) Occurs where the *Contractor* encounters physical conditions within the Site. Although noting the physical conditions and the weather on Site is not a contractual duty of the *Supervisor*, it is a traditional duty. 60.1(13) Occurs where the *Contractor* encounters weather conditions within the Site. Although noting the weather on Site is not a contractual duty of the *Supervisor*, it is a traditional duty. 60.1(16) Not providing materials, facilities and samples for tests and inspections as required by the Works Information (strictly for the *Employer*, but it is likely that the *Supervisor* will have significant input).
61.1 *Supervisor* giving an instruction and issuing a certificate	It is the *Project Manager* who is required to notify the *Contractor* of a compensation event where the *Supervisor* gives an instruction or issues a certificate. The *Project Manager* can also state that the event arises from a fault of the *Contractor*. This clause assumes that the *Project Manager* has knowledge of what the *Supervisor* does or does not do during the period of the contract. Although the *Supervisor* is required to copy all his certificates to the *Project Manager*, there is otherwise no contractual notice required regarding the *Supervisor*'s instructions or decisions. If the *Project Manager* wants to be aware of the *Supervisor*'s actions, especially those which could result in a compensation event, he can either (a) rely on the *Contractor* to notify as a compensation event the instructions and decisions of the *Supervisor*, or (b) put in place an arrangement to be notified of the *Supervisor*'s instructions or decisions. A third option, which does not directly involve the *Project Manager*, is for the *Supervisor* to put in place a routine action to copy to the *Project Manager* all of the *Supervisor*'s instructions, notifications and other communication which the *Supervisor* is required to communicate in a form that can be read, copied and recorded (clause 13.1). With regards to the first option, where the *Project Manager* relies on the *Contractor* to notify as a compensation event the certificates and instructions of the *Supervisor*, the compensation event does not fall away where the *Contractor* does not notify the compensation event (clause 61.3) and the event can therefore be notified at any time during the contract, even where the opportunity to assess the time and cost effects of the communication has been lost. Putting aside the requirement to act in a spirit of mutual trust and co-operation, where the *Project Manager* and the *Contractor* have open discussions with each other about matters that could affect the project, the *Project Manager* may wish to put in place communication requirements to keep himself up-to-date about the *Supervisor*'s actions. Likewise, the *Supervisor* may wish to initiate contact with the *Project Manager* about his actions and decisions.

ECC clause	*Supervisor* actions required
61.6 [The *Project Manager* is required] to state assumptions for the assessment of compensation events in the event that the effects are too uncertain to be forecast reasonably. [The *Project Manager* is required] to notify a correction to any assumptions later found to have been wrong. 62.1 [The *Project Manager* is required] to discuss with the *Contractor* different ways of dealing with the compensation event that are practicable.	The *Supervisor* is not contractually a part of the compensation event process – action is required only by the *Contractor* and the *Project Manager*. However, there is room for a *Project Manager* to accept advice and ideas from others, such as the *Supervisor*, when making decisions about compensation events.
71.1 [The *Supervisor* is required] to mark Equipment, Plant and Materials outside the Working Areas for payment purposes.	The title of Plant and Materials passes to the *Employer* when the Plant and Materials are brought within the Working Areas. However, the *Employer* can also gain the title of Plant and Materials outside the Working Areas if the *Supervisor* has marked them for the contract, that is they have been identified for payment and the *Contractor* has prepared them for marking in the way required by the Works Information. Careful attention should be paid to the process described in the Works Information as this affects the risk profile of the project. Equipment can be similarly marked for the contract, but the title does not pass to the *Employer* (unless there is a supplementary requirement through a Z clause or the Works Information). Note that title to Plant and Materials and the presence of Equipment on Site is mentioned in termination clauses 92 and 93.
82.1 Until the Defects Certificate, the *Contractor* replaces loss of and repairs damage to the *works*, Plant and Materials.	The *Contractor* is required to replace the loss of and to repair damage to the *works*, Plant and Materials at any point before the issue of the Defects Certificate. The timing of the issue of the Defects Certificate by the *Supervisor* therefore has a financial impact on the *Contractor*. As an aside, note that the *Contractor* is required to replace and repair 'promptly' and is not dependent on notification by the *Supervisor*; in other words, the *Contractor* is responsible for replacing loss of and repairing damage to the *works*, Plant and Materials.
84.2 The insurances provide cover until the Defects Certificate.	The timing of the issue of the Defects Certificate by the *Supervisor* has a financial impact on the *Contractor*.

ECC clause	*Supervisor* actions required	
W1 and W2 Dispute resolution	These clauses describing alternative dispute procedures are shown here merely to remind the *Supervisor* that there are consequences to the decisions he makes and his actions.	
	Option W1 W1.3(5) The *Adjudicator* may review and revise any action or inaction of the *Project Manager* or *Supervisor* related to the dispute. W1.3(9) Unless and until the *Adjudicator* has notified the Parties of his decision, the Parties, the *Project Manager* and the *Supervisor* proceed as if the matter disputed was not disputed. W1.4(4) The *tribunal* has the powers to review and revise any action or inaction of the *Project Manager* or the *Supervisor* related to the dispute.	**Option W2** W2.3(4) The *Adjudicator* may review and revise any action or inaction of the *Project Manager* or *Supervisor* related to the dispute. W2.3(9) Unless and until the *Adjudicator* has notified the Parties of his decision, the Parties, the *Project Manager* and the *Supervisor* proceed as if the matter disputed was not disputed. W2.4(3) The *tribunal* has the powers to … review and revise any action or inaction of the *Project Manager* or the *Supervisor* related to the dispute.
X12 Partnering	The *Supervisor* may be named as a Partner in the Schedule of Partners, in which case the *Supervisor* should familiarise himself with this option.	
X17 Low performance damages	The *Supervisor* is required to include in the Defects Certificate any Defect that shows a low performance compared with the performance level stated in the Contract Data.	
X20 Key Performance Indicators (not used with Option X12)	The *Supervisor* may be required to take part in the measuring and/or monitoring of the *Contractor*'s performance.	

NEC3: The Role of the *Supervisor*
ISBN 978-0-7277-6096-8

Agenda for a kick-off meeting between the *Supervisor* and the *Project Manager*

Issue (clause number)	Interpretation
▪ Form of communication during the project (13.1)	▪ How does the *Project Manager* wish the *Supervisor* to communicate to him [the *Project Manager*] and others, such as the *Contractor* and the *Employer*? ▪ Is there a project-specific format to use? ▪ Are there specific forms or a specific software package to use?
▪ *Period for reply* (13.3) ▪ Procedure for an extension to the *period for reply* (13.5)	▪ What is the standard *period for reply* going to be? ▪ What scope is there for the *Supervisor* to categorise the *period for reply* that affects him? ▪ What procedure does the *Project Manager* want to follow when the *Supervisor* wants to arrange an extension to his *period for reply* with the *Contractor*? ▪ What procedure does the *Project Manager* want to follow if the *Contractor* notifies a compensation event under clause 60.1(6) that the *Supervisor* did not communicate within the required parameters?
▪ Certificates to be copied to the *Project Manager* (13.6)	▪ Does the *Project Manager* want to receive copies of all communications from the *Supervisor* to the *Contractor* (rather than just the *Supervisor*'s certificates), or does the *Project Manager* want a regular meeting (e.g. once a week) to discuss all *Supervisor*-related issues, such as notified Defects?
▪ Notifying delegations (14.2)	▪ How would the *Project Manager* like to be informed if the *Supervisor* chooses to delegate some of his actions, for example the marking of Plant and Materials outside the Working Areas (clause 71.1).
▪ Replacing the *Supervisor* (14.4)	▪ The contract does not specify any actions regarding replacing the *Supervisor* other than the *Employer* advising the *Contractor* of the replacement before the replacement actually takes place. However, the *Supervisor* may wish to inform the *Project Manager* that the replacement is imminent and he can seek guidance from the *Project Manager* at an early meeting about the preferred procedure.

Issue (clause number)	Interpretation
■ Early warning (16)	■ Does the *Project Manager* want the *Supervisor* to tell him of any matters that the *Supervisor* feels could change the cost/price/performance of the *works*? ■ If so, should this information be notified formally, as a contractual notification? ■ Does the *Project Manager* want the *Supervisor* to attend every risk reduction meeting? ■ If not, should the *Supervisor* wait until he is instructed to attend? ■ How does the *Project Manager* intend to communicate any actions required of the *Supervisor* that are decided at the meeting?
■ Ambiguities and inconsistencies; illegal or impossible requirements (17 and 18)	■ Does the *Project Manager* want the *Supervisor* to be part of any discussions about changes to the Works Information? ■ If so, will the *Supervisor* attend a regular meeting at which the changes are a regular agenda item, or will the *Project Manager* instruct the *Supervisor* separately to attend a meeting specifically for the purposes of discussing any clause 17 and/or 18 matters?
■ Provide the Works (20.1)	■ Does the *Project Manager* want to involve the *Supervisor* in any pre-start meetings about the Works Information? Discussions could include tests and/or inspections to be carried out (clause 40.1). ■ If so, what is the procedure to follow (e.g. when, where and how many; how to deal with actions arising from the meetings)?
■ The *Contractor*'s design (21)	■ Does the *Project Manager* want the *Supervisor* to be involved in reviewing the *Contractor*'s design (this could simply be for the *Supervisor* to get early sight and familiarity of the documents)? ■ If so, what is the procedure?
■ Access to work being done and to Plant and Materials being stored (27.2)	■ Does the *Project Manager* want the *Supervisor* to communicate when he [the *Supervisor*] is accessing work being done away from the main programme or to Plant and Materials? ■ If so, what is the procedure to follow?
■ *Supervisor*'s instructions (27.3)	■ Does the *Project Manager* want the *Supervisor* to alert the *Project Manager* whenever he [the *Supervisor*] gives an instruction to the *Contractor*? ■ Does the *Project Manager* want to set up a regular meeting at which *Supervisor* instructions will be a regular agenda item?
■ Date of Completion (30.2)	■ Does the *Project Manager* want to set up a meeting and/or procedure to discuss when Completion has been reached? This could include a review of the Works Information and any Defects that would prevent the *Employer* from using the *works* and Others from doing their work.
■ The programme (31)	■ Does the *Project Manager* intend to include the *Supervisor* in regular programme meetings or discussions? ■ If not, how does the *Project Manager* intend to keep the *Supervisor* informed of matters affecting the programme so that the *Supervisor* can do his work without affecting the programme?

Issue (clause number)	Interpretation
■ Provision of materials, facilities and samples (40.2)	■ Does the *Project Manager* want the *Supervisor* to tell him, prior to the test/inspection, when facilities etc. will be required from the *Employer*? ■ If so, what procedure should the *Supervisor* follow, especially if tests are repeated and the provision of items is required a second time? ■ Does the *Project Manager* want the *Supervisor* to advise him of quantities or other measurements to materials, facilities and samples provided by the *Employer* so that the *Project Manager* can assess accurately the cost of repeating a test after a Defect is found?
■ Notification of tests/inspections (40.3)	■ Does the *Project Manager* want to receive a copy of the *Supervisor*'s notification to the *Contractor* that he [the *Supervisor*] is due to carry out a test? ■ Does the *Project Manager* want to receive a copy of the *Supervisor*'s notification to the *Contractor* of the results? ■ Does the *Project Manager* want to be notified when tests/inspections are to be repeated and also whether the *Employer* needs to provide items for a second test? ■ If so, should this take place test by test or at a regular meeting, even if just an agenda item at another regular meeting (such as a meeting about Defects)? Tests and inspections on which a payment depends may be of particular interest to the *Project Manager*. ■ The *Supervisor* should also advise the *Project Manager* of any procedures he has put in place with the *Contractor* to deal with repeated tests or inspections and discussions about correcting Defects so that the *Supervisor* is able to carry out the tests without unnecessary delay.
■ Watching tests (40.3)	■ Does the *Project Manager* want to put a procedure in place for instances where the *Supervisor* wants to watch an inspection carried out by the *Contractor* or any other tests or inspections that the *Contractor* plans to carry out which are not required by the Works Information or the applicable law?
■ Testing Plant and Materials before their entry to the Working Areas (41.1)	■ Does the *Project Manager* want to be notified when the *Supervisor* notifies the *Contractor* that Plant and Materials have passed their tests and inspections and can then be taken into the Working Areas?
■ Carrying out a search for a Defect (42.1)	■ Does the *Project Manager* want the *Supervisor* to notify him when he [the *Supervisor*] instructs the *Contractor* to search for a Defect? ■ Does the *Project Manager* want to be given an indication of what the search entails? ■ Does the *Project Manager* want to know the reasons for the search? ■ Does the *Project Manager* want to be advised that the search is required only because the *Contractor* did not give sufficient notice to the *Supervisor* that he was going to do work that would cover a required test/inspection? ■ Does the *Project Manager* want to know if the *Employer* is required to provide facilities for the search to take place? ■ Does the *Project Manager* want to know if there could be an impact on the Accepted Programme?

Issue (clause number)	Interpretation
■ Notifying Defects (42.2)	■ Does the *Project Manager* want to receive copies of notifications of Defects from (a) the *Supervisor* and (b) the *Contractor*? ■ Does the *Project Manager* want to be notified when Defects are corrected or that they will be corrected after Completion? ■ Does the *Project Manager* want these sorts of communications to be part of a regular meeting about Defects so that the *Supervisor* can communicate all aspects of the project related to tests, inspections and Defects?
■ Correction before the end of the *defect correction period* (43.2)	■ What scope will the *Project Manager* give the *Supervisor* to extend a *defect correction period*, such as when a search reveals a Defect or when the immediate correction of a Defect will be better for the project (budget, programme, performance) than for it to be corrected at Completion?
■ Defects Certificate (43.3)	■ Since the *Supervisor* is obliged to copy the Defects Certificate to the *Project Manager*, there is no need for further discussion on this matter. However, the *Supervisor* may prefer to communicate briefly with the *Project Manager* regarding this formal end to the project.
■ Access to the *works* after take over (43.4)	■ How does the *Project Manager* intend to communicate to the *Supervisor* that the *defect correction period* for a particular Defect cannot start until access and use have been provided to the *Contractor* from the *Employer*?
■ Accepting Defects (44)	■ How does the *Project Manager* intend to communicate to the *Supervisor* that a Defect is going to be accepted, that the Works Information has been changed to reflect this and that the Completion Date has changed?
■ *Contractor*'s failure to correct a Defect after take over (45.1)	■ How does the *Project Manager* intend to communicate to the *Supervisor* that the *Contractor* has not corrected the Defect within its *defect correction period*? ■ How does the *Project Manager* intend to involve the *Supervisor* in the procedure that follows?
■ *Employer* unable to give access to correct a Defect (45.2)	■ Where access cannot be provided to the *Contractor* to correct a Defect, how does the *Project Manager* intend to involve the *Supervisor* in the procedure that follows?
■ *Project Manager*'s assessment of the amount due (50.1)	■ Does the *Project Manager* want to discuss with the *Supervisor* the assessment of the amount due? ■ If so, how regularly and in what format?
■ Compensation events (60)	■ How does the *Project Manager* wish to be advised if the *Supervisor* has done something that could lead to a compensation event?
■ Notification (61.1)	■ Does the *Project Manager* want to receive copies of all documentation provided by the *Supervisor* to the *Contractor* (e.g. instructions, decisions, notification, other communications)?

Issue (clause number)	Interpretation
■ Assumptions for and ways of dealing with a compensation event (61.6 and 62.1)	■ Does the *Project Manager* want to involve the *Supervisor* in discussions about compensation procedures? ■ If so, what procedures/meetings are required?
■ Marking of Plant and Materials (71)	■ Does the *Project Manager* want to be advised by the *Supervisor* when items outside the Working Areas have been marked for payment purposes?
■ Low performance damages in the Defects Certificate (X17)	■ Does the *Project Manager* want early notification if the *Supervisor* intends to include low performance information in the Defects Certificate?
■ Key Performance Indicators (X20)	■ What procedures does the *Project Manager* want the *Supervisor* to follow with regards to the monitoring and measurement of performance in accordance with secondary Option X20?

NEC3: The Role of the *Supervisor*
ISBN 978-0-7277-6096-8

ICE Publishing: All rights reserved
http://dx.doi.org/10.1680/nectrs.60968.113

Appendix 3
Supervisor check-sheet

The tables included in this appendix are designed to serve as a check-sheet for the *Supervisor*, in recognition that he cannot contribute effectively if he is not able to provide information to the *Project Manager* etc.

Appendix 3A: Start-up meeting

1. Communications
   - Form of communication
   - Procedures for the *period for reply*
   - Document format and recipients
   - Delegation procedures
   - Early warning/risk reduction procedures
   - Review of and amendments to contract documents
   - Communication about day-to-day activities
   - Meetings with the *Contractor*

2. Regular meetings and agendas
   - Meetings about programme matters and the amount due
   - Early warning/risk reduction meeting
   - Meeting about Defects
   - Meeting to discuss possible compensation events

3. Procedures regarding tests and inspection
   - Tests/inspections on which a payment is conditional

4. Procedures about Defects
   - Requirements for clause 43.2 – correcting Defects before Completion
   - Procedure for extending/changing the *defect correction period*
   - Procedure to instruct an immediate correction of a Defect
   - Procedure for searches
   - Procedures about the acceptance of Defects
   - Defects affecting payment, the programme, the Works Information

5. Procedures about marking Plant and Materials
   - *Contractor*'s requirements

Appendix 3B: Meeting about Defects

1. List of Defects
   - Collated list of Defects: notified by the *Supervisor*; notified by the *Contractor*; notified after a search; result of failed test/inspection; required correction date (would have prevented *Employer* using the *works* or prevent Others from doing their work); actual correction date; *defect correction period* and where amended/lengthened by agreement; notified after take over; accepted.
   - Identified patterns of Defects to be addressed
   - Categories of Defects – is it working?
   - Comment on Defects that notified the failure of a test/inspection – effect on the programme; payment conditional on the passing of a test/inspection; assessing the cost of repeating a test/inspection.
   - List of Defects that will be accepted
   - List of instructed searches for Defects

2. Comments about the *defect correction period*
   - List of Defects for which the *defect correction period* was extended
   - List of Defects for which the *Supervisor* has required immediate correction
   - Is the idea of the *defect correction period* beginning at Completion working?
   - Are fewer/more Defect categories needed?
   - Are changes required?

3. Programme
   - Any Defects that are preventing the completion of an activity
   - Defects affecting Disallowed Cost (main Options C, D, E and F)

4. Payment
   - Tests or inspections upon which payments are conditional: any such tests/inspections which took place in the previous month that the *Project Manager* will have to take into account
   - Any such tests/inspections that are due in the forthcoming month

5. Accepting Defects
   - List of accepted Defects
   - Defects that the *Supervisor* thinks the *Project Manager* could propose acceptance to the *Contractor*

6. Searches
   - List of searches instructed and carried out and any resulting Defects
   - How the Defects were dealt with (accepted/corrected/changes to the Works Information)
   - Any patterns/trends with regards to searches
   - Impact on the programme

Appendix 3C: Monthly meeting between the *Supervisor* and the *Project Manager*

In this table, all general topics of discussion between the *Supervisor* and the *Project Manager* are listed, along with the ECC clauses from which the topics arise.

Agenda: monthly meeting between the *Supervisor* and the *Project Manager*

1. Tests/inspections before delivery   (Clause 41.1)
   - Plant and Materials which have passed tests and inspections and can be delivered to the Working Areas

2. Marking of Equipment, Plant and Materials outside the Working Areas   (Clause 71.1)
   - Equipment, Plant and Materials which are outside the Working Areas and which the *Supervisor* has marked for payment in accordance with the Works Information

3. Payment – discussion about whether activities are complete and about Disallowed Costs

   Option A (clause 11.2(27)); Option B (clause 11.2(28))
   - Activities or work that are/is complete, that is without Defects that would either delay or be covered by immediately following work

   Options C, D and E (clauses 11.2(23) and 11.2(25))
   - Defects to be corrected after Completion
   - Defects caused by the *Contractor* not complying with a constraint on how he is to Provide the Works stated in the Works Information

   Option D (clause 11.2(33))
   - Work that is complete, that is without Defects that would either delay or be covered by immediately following work

   Option F (clause 11.2(24))
   - Defects to be corrected after Completion

4. Early warnings and compensation events   (Clauses 16 and 60.1)
   - Discussions about early warnings and other risks
   - Any *Supervisor* actions that may be compensation events: *Supervisor* does not reply in time; *Supervisor* has changed a decision; a search was instructed and no Defect found; unnecessary delay on a test or inspection
   - Any changes to the Accepted Programme as a result of a compensation event which may affect the *Supervisor*'s duties or schedules

5. Site Information and records
   - Any discussions about Site Information recorded during the previous month

---

Appendix 3D: Template for a list of Defects

No.	Description	Notified by *Supervisor*	Notified by *Contractor*	Notified after a search	Failed test/inspection	Notified after take over	Will delay or be covered by immediately following work	Date notified	Would prevent *Employer* using the *works*	Would prevent Others doing their work	*defect correction period*	Amended *defect correction period*	Required correction date	Actual correction date	Accepted (date)	Closed
D1		✓														

NEC3: The Role of the *Supervisor*
ISBN 978-0-7277-6096-8

ICE Publishing: All rights reserved
http://dx.doi.org/10.1680/nectrs.60968.117

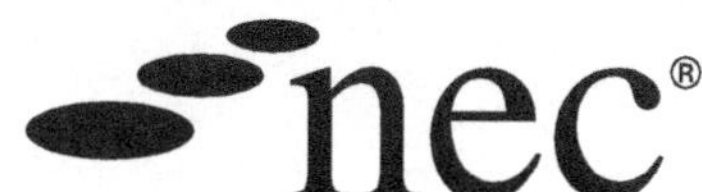

Appendix 4
Sample site diary

PEOPLE

Activity no:	Activity description	People (resource level)
Arrival:		
Removal:		
People standing idle (reason)		

EQUIPMENT

Arrival:	
Removal:	
List Equipment in Working Area	
Equipment standing idle (reason)	

PLANT AND MATERIALS

Arrival:	
Removal:	
Comments (storage/handling/etc)	

SUBCONTRACTORS

Activity no:	Activity description	Resources
Arrival:		
Removal:		
Standing time (reason)		

TESTS AND INSPECTIONS

List tests and inspections undertaken and witnessed:	
Other (describe)	

INCIDENTS ON SITE

Health and safety	
Public welfare	
Other (describe)	

COMMUNICATIONS

Project Manager's instructions:	
Supervisor's instructions:	
Early warning notification:	
Technical queries/answers:	
Drawings issued:	
Other (describe)	

OTHER EVENTS

Site visitors:	
Complaints:	

NEC3: The Role of the *Supervisor*
ISBN 978-0-7277-6096-8

ICE Publishing: All rights reserved
http://dx.doi.org/10.1680/nectrs.60968.119

Appendix 5
Supervisor notifications, instructions and certificate

The communication forms in this appendix can be used by *Supervisors* for the tasks indicated. These forms are provided as a guide only and may be adapted to suit the project and the parties involved.

Appendix 5A: *Supervisor*'s notification of delegation

<table>
<tr><td colspan="4" align="center">Supervisor's Notification of Delegation</td></tr>
<tr><td>From</td><td colspan="3">The Supervisor</td></tr>
<tr><td>To</td><td colspan="3">The Contractor</td></tr>
<tr><td>Contract Name:</td><td colspan="3">XYZ</td></tr>
<tr><td>Contract Ref:</td><td colspan="3">1234</td></tr>
<tr><td colspan="4">In accordance with Clause 14.2 of the conditions of contract, the following actions of the Supervisor are delegated to</td></tr>
<tr><td>[insert name]</td><td colspan="2">From [insert date]</td><td>To [insert date]</td></tr>
<tr><td>Clause</td><td colspan="2">Obligation/action</td><td>Delegated</td></tr>
<tr><td>10.1</td><td colspan="2">to act as stated in the contract and in a spirit of mutual trust and co-operation</td><td align="center">✓</td></tr>
<tr><td>13.1</td><td colspan="2">to communicate in a form which can be read, copied and recorded</td><td align="center">✓</td></tr>
<tr><td>13.3</td><td colspan="2">to reply to a communication within the period for reply</td><td align="center">✓</td></tr>
<tr><td>13.6</td><td colspan="2">to issue certificates to the Project Manager and the Contractor</td><td align="center">✓</td></tr>
<tr><td>40.3</td><td colspan="2">to notify the Contractor of his tests and inspections before they start and afterwards of the results</td><td></td></tr>
<tr><td>40.5</td><td colspan="2">to do tests and inspections without causing unnecessary delay</td><td></td></tr>
<tr><td>42.1</td><td colspan="2">to give reasons for searches which are instructed</td><td></td></tr>
<tr><td>42.2</td><td colspan="2">to notify the Contractor of Defects found</td><td></td></tr>
<tr><td>43.2</td><td colspan="2">to issue the Defects Certificate</td><td>Retained by the Supervisor</td></tr>
<tr><td>71.1</td><td colspan="2">to mark Equipment and Plant and Materials outside the Working Area for payment purposes if required by the contract.</td><td align="center">✓</td></tr>
<tr><td colspan="4"> </td></tr>
<tr><td>Signed Supervisor:</td><td colspan="3"></td></tr>
<tr><td>Dated:</td><td colspan="3"></td></tr>
<tr><td>Copied to:</td><td colspan="3">Employer; Project Manager</td></tr>
</table>

Appendix 5B: *Supervisor*'s Notification of cancellation of delegation

<table>
<tr><td colspan="4" align="center">Supervisor's Notification of Cancellation of Delegation</td></tr>
<tr><td>From</td><td colspan="3">The Supervisor</td></tr>
<tr><td>To</td><td colspan="3">The Contractor</td></tr>
<tr><td>Contract Name:</td><td colspan="3">XYZ</td></tr>
<tr><td>Contract Ref:</td><td colspan="3">1234</td></tr>
<tr><td>Document Ref:</td><td colspan="3">XYZ/1234/12</td></tr>
<tr><td colspan="4">In accordance with Clause 14.2 of the conditions of contract, this notification cancels the delegation of the following actions of the Supervisor to</td></tr>
<tr><td colspan="2">[insert name]</td><td>From [insert date]</td><td>To [insert date]</td></tr>
<tr><td>Clause</td><td colspan="2">Obligation/action</td><td>Delegated</td></tr>
<tr><td>10.1</td><td colspan="2">to act as stated in the contract and in a spirit of mutual trust and co-operation</td><td align="center">✓</td></tr>
<tr><td>13.1</td><td colspan="2">to communicate in a form which can be read, copied and recorded</td><td align="center">✓</td></tr>
<tr><td>13.3</td><td colspan="2">to reply to a communication within the period for reply</td><td align="center">✓</td></tr>
<tr><td>13.6</td><td colspan="2">to issue certificates to the Project Manager and the Contractor</td><td align="center">✓</td></tr>
<tr><td>40.3</td><td colspan="2">to notify the Contractor of his tests and inspections before they start and afterwards of the results</td><td></td></tr>
<tr><td>40.5</td><td colspan="2">to do tests and inspections without causing unnecessary delay</td><td></td></tr>
<tr><td>42.1</td><td colspan="2">to give reasons for searches which are instructed</td><td></td></tr>
<tr><td>42.2</td><td colspan="2">to notify the Contractor of Defects found</td><td></td></tr>
<tr><td>43.2</td><td colspan="2">to issue the Defects Certificate</td><td align="center">Retained by the Supervisor</td></tr>
<tr><td>71.1</td><td colspan="2">to mark Equipment and Plant and Materials outside the Working Area for payment purposes if required by the contract.</td><td align="center">✓</td></tr>
<tr><td colspan="4"> </td></tr>
<tr><td colspan="2">Signed Supervisor:</td><td colspan="2"></td></tr>
<tr><td colspan="2">Dated:</td><td colspan="2"></td></tr>
<tr><td colspan="2">Copied to:</td><td colspan="2">Employer; Project Manager</td></tr>
</table>

Appendix 5C: *Supervisor*'s notification

Reproduced with permission from *NEC3: How to Use the ECC Communication Forms* (ISBN 978-0-7277-5909-2), available at www.neccontract.com.

<table>
<tr><td colspan="2" align="right">***Supervisor*'s Notification**
For use with ECC</td></tr>
<tr><td>To:</td><td>Date:</td></tr>
<tr><td>Project Name:</td><td>Project ID:</td></tr>
<tr><td>Notification No:</td><td></td></tr>
<tr><td colspan="2">Under clause ______ I notify you:</td></tr>
<tr><td>Copy to:</td><td></td></tr>
<tr><td>Signed:</td><td></td></tr>
<tr><td>For:</td><td>Date:</td></tr>
</table>

Appendix 5D: *Contractor's* notification

Reproduced with permission from *NEC3: How to Use the ECC Communication Forms* (ISBN 978-0-7277-5909-2), available at www.neccontract.com.

<table>
<tr><td colspan="2" align="right">Contractor's Notification
For use with ECC</td></tr>
<tr><td>To:</td><td>Date:</td></tr>
<tr><td>Project Name:</td><td>Project ID:</td></tr>
<tr><td>Notification No:</td><td></td></tr>
<tr><td colspan="2">Under clause _______ I notify you:</td></tr>
<tr><td>Copy to:</td><td></td></tr>
<tr><td>Signed:</td><td></td></tr>
<tr><td>For:</td><td>Date:</td></tr>
</table>

Appendix 5E: Defects Certificate

Reproduced with permission from *NEC3: How to Use the ECC Communication Forms* (ISBN 978-0-7277-5909-2), available at www.neccontract.com.

<table>
<tr><td colspan="2" align="right">Defects Certificate
For use with ECC</td></tr>
<tr><td>To: ____________________</td><td>Date: ____________________</td></tr>
<tr><td>Project Name: ____________________</td><td>Project ID: ____________________</td></tr>
<tr><td>Certificate No: ____________________</td><td></td></tr>
<tr><td colspan="2">Under clause 43.3/11.2(6):

[either] there are no Defects notified before the defects date which the Contractor
has not corrected.
[or] the following is a list of Defects notified before the defects date which the
Contractor has not corrected:

</td></tr>
<tr><td colspan="2">Copy to: ____________________

Signed: ____________________</td></tr>
<tr><td>For: ____________________</td><td>Date: ____________________</td></tr>
</table>

Defects Certificate

To: **Mr K Williams, Greenwheat County Council**   Date: **14th October 2015**

Project Name: **Much Binding Bypass**   Project ID: **1234**

Certificate No: **1**

Under clause 43.3/11.2(6):

there are no Defects notified before the *defects date* which the *Contractor* has

not corrected.

Copy to: **D Cameron, Woodstone Construction Ltd**

Signed: H. Paddick.

For: **Greenwheat County Council**   Date: **14th October 2015**

Appendix 5F: *Supervisor*'s instruction

Reproduced with permission from *NEC3: How to Use the ECC Communication Forms* (ISBN 978-0-7277-5909-2), available at www.neccontract.com.

<table>
<tr><td colspan="2" align="right">***Supervisor*'s Instruction**
For use with ECC</td></tr>
<tr><td>To:</td><td>Date:</td></tr>
<tr><td>Project Name:</td><td>Project ID:</td></tr>
<tr><td>Instruction No:</td><td></td></tr>
<tr><td colspan="2">Under clause _____ I instruct you to:</td></tr>
<tr><td>Copy to:</td><td></td></tr>
<tr><td>Signed:</td><td></td></tr>
<tr><td>For:</td><td>Date:</td></tr>
</table>

Supervisor's Instruction

To: **D Cameron, Woodstone Construction Ltd**   Date: **14th September 2015**

Project Name: **Much Binding Bypass**   Project ID: **1234**

Instruction No: **1**

Under clause 42.1 I instruct you to:

Uncover the drain run MH1–MH2 as the attached sketch XYZ to allow

inspection/testing by me. The reason for the search is that local settlement appears

to be taking place.

Copy to: **Site Team**

Signed: *H. Paddick.*

For: **Greenwheat County Council**   Date: **14th September 2015**

Appendix 5G: *Contractor*'s notification of test/inspection and results

Reproduced with permission from *NEC3: How to Use the ECC Communication Forms* (ISBN 978-0-7277-5909-2), available at www.neccontract.com.

Contractor's Notification of a test/inspection and results		
From	The *Contractor*	
To	The *Supervisor*	
Contract Name:	XYZ	
Contract Ref:	1234	
Test/inspection notification no:	XYZ/1234/12	Date:
The following test/inspection will be carried out [date and time]:		
By:		
Reference in the Works Information/law:		
Part of the Site:		
Materials, facilities and samples are required as follows:		
This area will/will not be obstructed by following work.		
Signed *Contractor*:		
Dated:		
Copied to:		
Test result:		
Signed by the *Contractor*:	Date:	

Appendix 5H: *Supervisor*'s notification of test/inspection and results

Supervisor's Notification of a test/inspection and results	
From	The *Supervisor*
To	The *Contractor*
Contract Name:	XYZ
Contract Ref:	1234
Test/inspection notification no:	XYZ/1234/12 Date:
The following test/inspection will be carried out [date and time]:	
By:	
Reference in the Works Information/law:	
Part of the Site:	
Materials, facilities and samples are required as follows:	
This area will/will not be obstructed by following work.	
Signed *Supervisor*:	
Dated:	
Copied to:	
Test result:	
Signed by the *Supervisor*: Date:	

Appendix 5I: *Supervisor*'s notification of a Defect

Supervisor's **Notification**

To: **D Cameron, Woodstone Construction Ltd**   Date: **31st August 2015**

Project Name: **Much Binding Bypass**   Project ID: **1234**

Notification No: **1**

Under clause 42.2 I notify you:

that the brickwork to the cycle store is not in accordance with the

Works Information.

Copy to: **Site Team**

Signed: *H. Paddick.*

For: **Greenwheat County Council**   Date: **31st August 2015**

Appendix 5J: *Contractor*'s notification of a Defect

<table>
<tr><td colspan="2" align="right">***Contractor*'s Notification**</td></tr>
<tr><td>To: **Mr H Paddick, Greenwheat County Council**</td><td>Date: **24th August 2015**</td></tr>
<tr><td>Project Name: **Much Binding Bypass**</td><td>Project ID: **1234**</td></tr>
<tr><td>Notification No: **2**</td><td></td></tr>
<tr><td colspan="2">Under clause 42.2 I notify you:

that we have tested drain run A–B and found what appears to be a collapse.

This is a Defect and we intend to correct this shortly.</td></tr>
<tr><td colspan="2">Copy to: **Site Team, Head Office**</td></tr>
<tr><td colspan="2">Signed:</td></tr>
<tr><td>For: **Woodstone Construction Ltd**</td><td>Date: **24th August 2015**</td></tr>
</table>

NEC3: The Role of the *Supervisor*
ISBN 978-0-7277-6096-8

ICE Publishing: All rights reserved
http://dx.doi.org/10.1680/nectrs.60968.133

Appendix 6
Checklist and reminders

Appendix 6A: *Supervisor*'s checklist

Project title	
starting date	
Completion Date	
Key Dates	
sectional *completion dates*	
period for reply	
defects date	
defect correction period	
Works Information	
Site Information	
Risk Register	
Accepted Programme	
Activity Schedule/Bill of Quantities	
Works Information for the *Contractor*'s design	
Working Areas	
Z clauses	

Appendix 6B: Checklist for documents required by the Works Information

EU legislation/regulations	
UK legislation/regulations	
British Standards	
Guidance required by the *Employer*	

NEC3: The Role of the *Supervisor*
ISBN 978-0-7277-6096-8

Appendix 7
Quick reference guide and glossary

Appendix 7A: Quick reference guide

Clause	Express duties
10.1	to act as stated in the contract and in a spirit of mutual trust and co-operation
13.1	to communicate in a form which can be read, copied and recorded
13.3	to reply to a communication within the *period for reply*
13.6	to issue certificates to the *Project Manager* and to the *Contractor* (Defects Certificate)
14.2	to notify the *Contractor* before delegating any actions or cancelling any delegation
40.3	to notify the *Contractor* of his tests and inspections before they start and afterwards of the results
40.5	to do tests and inspections without causing unnecessary delay to work or payment
41.1	to notify the *Contractor* of results of tests on or inspections of Plant and Materials required by Works Information before delivery can take place
42.1	to instruct searches and to give reasons for those searches (note clause 60.1(10): The *Supervisor* instructs the *Contractor* to search for a Defect and no Defect is found unless the search is needed only because the Contractor gave insufficient notice of doing the work obstructing a required test or inspection)
42.2	to notify the *Contractor* of Defects found before the *defects date*
43.3	to issue the Defects Certificate
71.1	to mark Equipment and Plant and Materials outside the Working Areas for payment purposes

Appendix 7B: Glossary
The *Supervisor*'s essential glossary of identified and defined terms

(Note: the following are the standard ECC definitions and you should check for amendments in each specific contract.)

Identified terms in the ECC Contract Data part one – Data provided by the *Employer*	
1 General	■ The Works Information is in . . . . . . [the document entitled 'Works Information'] ■ The *language of the contract* is . . . ■ The *period for reply* is . . .

4 Testing and Defects	■ The *defects date* is . . . . . . weeks after Completion of the whole of the *works*.
	■ The *defect correction period* is . . . . . . weeks except that
	  – the *defect correction period* for . . . . . . is . . . . . . weeks
	  – the *defect correction period* for . . . . . . is . . . . . . weeks
	  – the *defect correction period* for . . . . . . is . . . . . . weeks.

Identified terms in the ECC Contract Data part two – Data provided by the *Contractor*	
1 General	■ The Works Information for the *Contractor*'s design is in . . . . . . [the document entitled '*Contractor*'s Works Information'].

Definitions in the ECC	How they affect the *Supervisor*
11.2(2) Completion is when the *Contractor* has ■ done all the work which the Works Information states he is to do by the Completion Date and ■ corrected notified Defects which would have prevented the *Employer* from using the *works* and Others from doing their work. If the work that the *Contractor* is to do by the Completion Date is not stated in the Works Information, Completion is when the *Contractor* has done all the work necessary for the *Employer* to use the *works* and for Others to do their work.	The *Supervisor* is responsible for notifying Defects and therefore the *Supervisor* can affect the status of Completion, which is decided by the *Project Manager*.
11.2(3) The Completion Date is the *completion date* unless later changed in accordance with this contract.	The *Supervisor* works with the Works Information in his notifying of Defects and his carrying out and watching of tests and inspections and therefore has to be aware of the Completion Date.
11.2(5) A Defect is ■ a part of the *works* which is not in accordance with the Works Information or ■ a part of the *works* designed by the *Contractor* which is not in accordance with the applicable law or the *Contractor*'s design which the *Project Manager* has accepted.	The *Supervisor* notifies Defects until the *defects date* and therefore needs to understand the definition of a Defect.

Definitions in the ECC	How they affect the *Supervisor*
11.2(6) The Defects Certificate is either a list of Defects that the *Supervisor* has notified before the *defects date* which the *Contractor* has not corrected or, if there are no such Defects, a statement that there are none.	The *Supervisor* issues the Defects Certificate and needs to understand what it comprises and when it is to be issued.
11.2(7) Equipment is items provided by the *Contractor* and used by him to Provide the Works and which the Works Information does not require him to include in the *works*.	The *Supervisor* may need to mark Equipment that is outside the Working Areas.
11.2(9) A Key Date is the date by which work is to meet the Condition stated. The Key Date is the *key date* stated in the Contract Data and the Condition is the *condition* stated in the Contract Data unless later changed in accordance with this contract.	The Key Dates affect the Accepted Programme, to which the *Contractor*, the *Project Manager* and the *Supervisor* all work.
11.2(10) Others are people or organisations who are not the *Employer*, the *Project Manager*, the *Supervisor*, the *Adjudicator*, the *Contractor* or any employee, Subcontractor or supplier of the *Contractor*.	The *Supervisor* may be required to work with Others where stated in the Works Information and the *Supervisor*'s personal contract, for example a health and safety inspector.
11.2(12) Plant and Materials are items to be included in the *works*.	The *Supervisor* may need to mark Plant and Materials that are outside the Working Areas.
11.2(13) To Provide the Works means to do the work necessary to complete the *works* in accordance with this contract and all incidental work, services and actions which this contract requires.	The *Contractor*, the *Project Manager* and the *Supervisor* all need to understand what is required to complete the *works*.
11.2(15) The Site is the area within the *boundaries of the site* and the volumes above and below it which are affected by the work included in this contract.	The *Contractor*, the *Project Manager* and the *Supervisor* all need to understand where the Site is.
11.2(16) The Site Information is information which ■ describes the Site and its surroundings and ■ is in the documents which the Contract Data states it is in.	The *Contractor*, the *Project Manager* and the *Supervisor* all need to understand the information about the Site.
11.2(17) A Subcontractor is a person or organisation who has a contract with the *Contractor* to ■ construct or install a part of the *works*, ■ provide a service necessary to Provide the Works or ■ supply Plant and Materials which the person or organisation has wholly or partly designed for the *works*.	The *Supervisor* notifies Defects and carries out or watches tests or inspections and therefore needs to know who the Subcontractors are and what work they will be undertaking.
11.2(18) The Working Areas are those parts of the *working areas* which are ■ necessary for Providing the Works and ■ used only for work in this contract unless later changed in accordance with this contract.	As well as the Site, the *Supervisor* needs to understand where the Working Areas are so that he can mark as required the Equipment, Plant and Materials which are outside the Working Areas.

Definitions in the ECC	How they affect the *Supervisor*
11.2(19) The Works Information is information which either ■ specifies and describes the *works* or ■ states any constraints on how the *Contractor* Provides the Works and is either ■ in the documents which the Contract Data states it is in or ■ in an instruction given in accordance with this contract.	The *Supervisor* must work closely with the Works Information so that he can notify Defects (a part of the *works* which are not in accordance with the Works Information) and carry out and watch tests and inspections as well as mark relevant items.

Clause number	Clause extracted from the ECC
Clause 13.1	Each … notification … which this contract requires is communicated in a form which can be read, copied and recorded.
Clause 13.6	The *Supervisor* issues his certificates to the *Project Manager* and the *Contractor*. [Quoted to show that the contract does not require notifications to be distributed.]
Clause 13.7	A notification which this contract requires is communicated separately from other communications.
Clause 35.1	… the *Employer* takes over the *works* not later than two weeks after Completion.
Clause 35.2	[If the *Employer* uses any part of the *works* before Completion has been certified] he takes over the part of the *works* when he begins to use it except if the use is …
Clause 35.3	The *Project Manager* certifies the date upon which the Employer takes over … within one week of the date [of take over].
Clause 40.1	This clause only applies to tests and inspections required by the Works Information or the applicable law.
Clause 40.2	The *Contractor* and the *Employer* provide materials, facilities and samples for tests and inspections as stated in the Works Information.
Clause 40.3	The *Contractor* and the *Supervisor* each notifies the other of each of his tests and inspections before it starts and afterwards notifies the other of its results. The *Contractor* notifies the *Supervisor* in time for a test or inspection to be arranged and done before doing work which would obstruct the test or inspection. The *Supervisor* may watch any test done by the *Contractor*.
Clause 40.4	If a test or inspection shows that any work has a Defect, the *Contractor* corrects the Defect and the test or inspection is repeated.
Clause 40.5	The *Supervisor* does his tests and inspections without causing unnecessary delay to work or to a payment which is conditional upon a test or inspection being successful. A payment which is conditional upon a *Supervisor's* test or inspection being successful becomes due at the later of the *defects date* and the end of the last *defect correction period* if ■ the *Supervisor* has not done the test or inspection and ■ the delay to the test or inspection is not the *Contractor's* fault.
Clause 40.6	The *Project Manager* assesses the cost incurred by the *Employer* in repeating a test or inspection after a Defect is found. The *Contractor* pays the amount assessed.
Clause 41.1	The *Contractor* does not bring to the Working Areas those Plant and Materials which the Works Information states are to be tested or inspected before delivery until the *Supervisor* has notified the *Contractor* that they have passed the test or inspection.
Clause 42.1	Until the *defects date*, the *Supervisor* may instruct the *Contractor* to search for a Defect. He gives his reason for the search with his instruction. Searching may include ■ uncovering, dismantling, re-covering and re-erecting works, ■ providing facilities, materials and samples for tests and inspections done by the *Supervisor* and ■ doing tests and inspections which the Works Information does not require.

Clause number	Clause extracted from the ECC
Clause 42.2	Until the *defects date*, the *Supervisor* notifies the *Contractor* of each Defect as soon as he finds it and the *Contractor* notifies the *Supervisor* of each Defect as soon as he finds it.
Clause 43.1	The *Contractor* corrects a Defect whether or not the *Supervisor* notifies him of it.
Clause 43.2	The *Contractor* corrects a notified Defect before the end of the *defect correction period*. The *defect correction period* begins at Completion for Defects notified before Completion and when the Defect is notified for other Defects.
Clause 43.3	The *Supervisor* issues the Defects Certificate at the later of the *defects date* and the end of the last *defect correction period*. The *Employer*'s rights in respect of a Defect which the *Supervisor* has not found or notified are not affected by the issue of the Defects Certificate.
Clause 43.4	The *Project Manager* arranges for the *Employer* to allow the *Contractor* access to and use of a part of the *works* which he has taken over if they are needed for correcting a Defect. In this case, the *defect correction period* begins when the necessary access and use of the *works* have been provided.
Clause 44.1	The *Contractor* and the *Project Manager* may propose to the other that the Works Information should be changed so that a Defect does not have to be corrected.
Clause 44.2	If the *Contractor* and the *Project Manager* are prepared to consider the change, the *Contractor* submits a quotation for reduced Prices or an earlier Completion Date or both to the *Project Manager* for acceptance. If the *Project Manager* accepts the quotation, he gives an instruction to change the Works Information, the Prices and the Completion Date accordingly.
Clause 45.1	If the *Contractor* is given access in order to correct a notified Defect but he has not corrected it within its *defect correction period*, the *Project Manager* assesses the cost to the *Employer* of having the Defect corrected by other people and the *Contractor* pays this amount. The Works Information is treated as having been changed to accept the Defect.
Clause 45.2	If the *Contractor* is not given access in order to correct a notified Defect before the *defects date*, the *Project Manager* assesses the cost to the *Contractor* of correcting the Defect and the *Contractor* pays this amount. The Works Information is treated as having been changed to accept the Defect.
Clause 60.1(3)	The *Employer* does not provide something which he is to provide by the date for providing it shown on the Accepted Programme.
Clause 60.1(6)	… the *Supervisor* does not reply to a communication from the *Contractor* within the period required by the contract.
Clause 60.1(8)	The … *Supervisor* changes a decision which he had previously communicated.
Clause 60.1(10)	The *Supervisor* instructs the *Contractor* to search for a Defect and no Defect is found unless the search is needed only because the *Contractor* gave insufficient notice of doing work obstructing a required test or inspection.
Clause 60.1(11)	A test or inspection by the *Supervisor* causes unnecessary delay.
Clause 60.1(16)	The *Employer* does not provide materials, facilities and samples for tests and inspections as stated in the Works Information.
Clause 70.1	Whatever title the *Contractor* has to Plant and Materials which is outside the Working Areas passes to the *Employer* if the *Supervisor* has marked it as for this contract.
Clause 71.1	The *Supervisor* marks Equipment, Plant and Materials which are outside the Working Areas if ■ this contract identifies them for payment and ■ the *Contractor* has prepared them for marking as the Works Information requires.

NEC3: The Role of the *Supervisor*
ISBN 978-0-7277-6096-8

ICE Publishing: All rights reserved
http://dx.doi.org/10.1680/nectrs.60968.141

Index